This fine and important study provides readers with a first-class treatment of the role of microfinance in Christian mission. Ronsen is very well placed to write this, as someone with long experience and strong expertise in microfinance. He has given us a thoughtful and engaging book which locates microfinance within a holistic view of Christian mission, rooted in the Lausanne Movement's concern for integral mission. He also provides two excellent in-depth case studies of the strengths and challenges of Christian microfinance in developing world contexts. This book will inform, engage, provoke and inspire readers: I commend it most warmly.

Steve Walton
Professor of New Testament,
St Mary's University, Twickenham, London, UK

I0081424

Global Perspectives Series

Mission Drift?

Langham
GLOBAL LIBRARY

Mission Drift?

Exploring a Paradigm Shift in Evangelical Mission with Particular Reference to Microfinance

Oddvar Sten Ronsen

Langham

GLOBAL LIBRARY

Published 2016 by Langham Global Library
an imprint of Langham Creative Projects

Langham Partnership
PO Box 296, Carlisle, Cumbria CA3 9WZ, UK
www.langham.org

ISBNs:
978-1-78368-095-5 Print
978-1-78368-090-0 Mobi
978-1-78368-089-4 ePub
978-1-78368-091-7 PDF

British Library Cataloguing in Publication Data
A catalogue record for this book is available from the British Library

ISBN: 978-1-78368-095-5

Cover & Book Design: projectluz.com

CONTENTS

Abstract

Many Christian missions have included microfinance in their integral mission work as a tool to help poor people break out of the poverty cycle. This study analyses the extent to which Christian microfinance organizations are able to serve the poor materially and spiritually by employing microfinance as a platform for Christian integral mission. I argue that although a basic theological consensus that social action and evangelism are inextricably linked to each other has emerged in the evangelical church, the perennial debate as to whether evangelism should have "priority" over social action has led to a lack of conceptual clarity and loss of direction in integral mission. I propose that the concept of "anticipated" evangelism should replace that of the "priority" of evangelism to reflect the fact that social action and evangelism do not necessarily coincide in time but that the interlinkage between them should be carefully planned. The concept of "mission drift" is introduced to indicate how Christian microfinance that originally intended to serve the social and spiritual needs of the poor may over time become relatively unrelated to the proclamation of the gospel. The viability of microfinance as a platform for Christian integral mission is appraised in a field study in the Philippines and Thailand. The case study relates to the two standard bottom lines of microfinance – that is, whether the operations are financially sustainable and whether they can deliver a social good to the poor. In addition the study relates to a third bottom line which is whether Christian microfinance can also be integral mission and a bridge for the gospel. The field study also sheds light on risk factors that can produce mission drift in relation to the objectives of integral mission and indicates how these may be handled. The case studies demonstrate that the ability of Christian microfinance to deliver a social good to the poor through microfinance is not incompatible with using microfinance as a platform for evangelism, provided the microfinance organizations are aware of and willing to handle the mechanisms that produce mission drift.

Abbreviations

APPEND	Alliance of Philippine Partners in Enterprise Development
CCT	Centre for Community Transformation
CFI	Common Interest Foundation
CGAP	Consultative Group to Assist the Poorest
CMED	Christian microenterprise development
CRESR	International Consultation on the Relationship between Evangelism and Social Responsibility
CRS	Catholic Relief Services
ICOWE	International Congress on World Evangelization
MCP	Microfinance Council of the Philippines
MED	Microenterprise development
MEDA	Mennonite Economic Development Association
MFO	Microfinance organization
MIX	Microfinance Information Exchange
NGO	Non-governmental organization
NMA	Norwegian Mission Alliance
NT	New Testament
OECD	Organization for Economic Cooperation and Development
OI	Opportunity International
OT	Old Testament
PHP	Philippine Peso
SA	Step Ahead
TDF	Transformational Development Framework
THB	Thai Baht
WEF	World Evangelical Fellowship

1

Introduction

In the course of the last three decades the concept of integral mission,[1] also called holistic mission,[2] has become the dominating basis for most Christian mission agencies. As a part of this trend microfinance found its way into Christian mission activities. Previously missions had incorporated health services, hospital operations, orphanages, and so on, into their activities, but up to then not traditional instruments of finance aimed at helping people to break out of the poverty cycle by extending to them small loans for micro-enterprises. When microcredit was launched with the promise of changing the lives of millions of poor people around the world by giving them access to capital from which they had hitherto been precluded, many Christian NGOs,[3] agencies and missions adopted it. This tended to fit well into their focus on poor and impoverished groups in the countries in which they worked. The age of microfinance came with the introduction of other financial products, such as voluntary savings and insurance, that were offered to the clients.

Microfinance was conceptually new and caught the interest of younger donor generations that embraced it as a way to impact the lives of the borrowers and their families directly through help to self-help, thereby creating self-sustaining community structures that could permanently improve their life conditions. However, measuring the effects of microfinance has turned out

---

1. "Integral mission" is a translation of the Spanish term *misión integral*, which originated in Latin America.

2. In this document "holistic mission" is used interchangeably with "integral mission." Both concepts reflect the need for Christian mission to embrace the wholeness of human beings.

3. Non-governmental organizations (NGOs) may have different kinds of structures, but common to them all is that they target some arena of social action and mobilize funds, both private and public, to ensure financial support for their activities.

to be a controversial issue in the microfinance industry, and some observers contend that the gap between microcredit rhetoric and reality is widening.[4]

The decisions by Christian agencies to launch microcredit were, however, generally made on a rather rudimentary basis. At the time little was known about the effects of microfinance on the poor client groups that were included in the operations, or about the implications of introducing microfinance into their mission work on the maintenance of commitment to the core values of the mission and the cohesion in the organization as the work expanded.[5] As some time has passed since then it is now possible to take a closer look at microfinance and consider whether it is justified to include microfinance in Christian mission work. If it is, how should it be structured and operated in relation to the overall mission work and the work of the church at large in order to satisfy basic conceptual requirements of integral mission theology?

In this study microfinance as a part of Christian mission work is considered in three dimensions. In the rapidly growing literature on microfinance the main hurdle of microfinance operations tends to be the need to demonstrate that the microfinance enterprise documents a double bottom line – that it is both financially sustainable and produces a social good for the poor. It is the contention in this paper that microfinance in Christian mission work should also demonstrate that the proclamation part of integral mission is maintained. This may be called the third bottom line in Christian microfinance operations. Some might argue that the double bottom line is in itself a daunting challenge, and to add the third dimension of proclamation[6] and evangelism[7] makes the challenge of microfinance in Christian mission even more demanding.

One key area of research is therefore to investigate important theological aspects of microfinance as an integral part of Christian mission. The study will particularly relate to issues connected with "mission drift." A dictionary definition of "drift" is "a gradual deviation from an original course, model,

---

4. Richard L. Meyer, as cited in Thomas Dichter and Malcolm Harper, *What's Wrong with Microfinance?* (Rugby: Intermediate Technology Publications, 2007), 225.

5. James F. Engel and William A. Dyrness, *Changing the Mind of Missions: Where Have We Gone Wrong?* (Downers Grove: IVP, 2000), 148.

6. In this study the word "proclamation" is used in the sense of proclaiming the historical biblical Christ as Saviour and Lord.

7. By "evangelism" is meant "the proclamation of the historical biblical Christ as Saviour and Lord, with a view to persuading people to come to him personally and so be reconciled to God." John Stott, *Making Christ Known: Historic Mission Documents from the Lausanne Movement 1974–1989* (Grand Rapids: Eerdmans, 1996), 28.

method or intention."[8] This general understanding of the meaning of "drift" has been widely adopted by the microfinance industry as it uses the concept of mission drift to describe how microfinance institutions often gradually drift away from serving the poor in order to maintain financial sustainability.[9] Another writer defines mission drift in microfinance in the same vein: "institutions that once served the poor move up market, abandoning the poor."[10] Mission drift is today a phenomenon of much concern in the microfinance industry as many have witnessed it around the world.[11] In the present study the concept of "mission drift" will also be applied to describe the extent to which microfinance activities run by Christian mission organizations may become relatively unrelated to the Christian context and the proclamation of the gospel and thus drift away from integral mission objectives, which are both to serve the poor and to proclaim the Christian gospel.

Mission drift in relation to the focus on the poor is of course also a topic of key interest in Christian microfinance. Microfinance is an unproven and immature field and it is today debated whether microfinance operations can produce a social good and at the same time be financially sustainable.[12] In order to ensure the profitability and sustainability of the operations some agencies have used methods that have the common feature of reducing the impact on the poor client groups. One approach has been to increase the average loan size to focus on more credit-worthy client groups (and thus move up the poverty ladder, leaving the poorer groups behind), or to reduce the extent of social service activities for clients when those services are not directly contributing to the profitability of the microfinance enterprise. Furthermore, commercial banking practices are increasingly being introduced in the form of state-of-the-art microfinance practice spearheaded by CGAP (Consultative Group to Assist the Poorest), some of which may not always be easy to reconcile with Christian mission objectives. After all, the extension of a credit also represents a debt at the hand of the borrower. Debt must be repaid. The relationship between the lender and the borrower is

---

8. The Free Dictionary, http//:www.thefreedictionary.com/drift; accessed 4 November 2010.

9. Roy Mersland and Øystein Strøm, "Microfinance Mission Drift? Description and Explanation," *World Development* 38, no. 1 (2010): 28–36; Elserver, www.elserver.com/locate/worlddev; accessed on 4 November 2010.

10. J. D. Von Pischke in Dichter and Harper, *What's Wrong with Microfinance?*, 143.

11. Carlos Danel, "Are We drifting Yet?," CGAP, 25 October 2010, http://microfinance.cgap.org/2010/10/25/are-we-drifting-yet/; accessed 4 November 2010.

12. Thomas Dichter, in Dichter and Harper, *What's Wrong with Microfinance?*, 4.

impacted and this may at times come into direct conflict with the endeavours to communicate the gospel. The consequences for individuals who do not repay may be tragic.

Critical articles have appeared in the media about small farmers in India who commit suicide as they are unable to pay, and the social ostracism that engulfs poor women who are unable to repay the loans which their solidarity group must then pay for them.[13] It was indeed a signal that the sentiment toward microfinance was changing when one of the major global microfinance capital providers, the Catholic Relief Services (CRS), decided to divest its holdings in microcredit in favour of savings-led microfinance due to a lack of conviction in the agency that the money spent on microcredit had the desired social impact.[14]

The main emphasis in this study is, however, related to some other major tendencies in microfinance operations run by Christian missions today. These may result in "mission drift" in relation to the proclamation of the gospel,[15] which parts of the evangelical church, especially in the period after the Second World War, tended to perceive as constituting the leading objective and *raison d'être* of Christian mission work.[16]

First, there are indications that microfinance operations are for various reasons gradually being separated from the work of the local church.[17] Second, the sheer numerical growth and increased competition in the microfinance market has brought more finance and marketing professionals into the microfinance work of the Christian missions, and they are not necessarily committed to the Christian faith. This may make it difficult to maintain a wholehearted acceptance of core values throughout the organization. It is quite probable that the overall effect of these two factors will be a growing

13. For example, Thilo Kunzemann, "Is Micro-finance a Debt Trap?," Allianz, http://knowledge.allianz.com/en/globalissues/microfinance/microcredit/microfinance_debt_trap.html; accessed 14 March 2010; or Ketaki Gokhale, "A Global Surge in Tiny Loans Spurs Credit Bubble in a Slum," *Wall Street Journal*, 13 August 2009, Allianz, http://knowledge.allianz.com/en/globalissues/microfinance/microcredit/microfinance_debt_trap.html; accessed 30 August 2010.

14. Kim Wilson, "The Moneylender's Dilemma," in Dichter and Harper, *What's Wrong with Microfinance?*, 98.

15. E.g. Ken Eldred, *God Is at Work, Transforming People and Nations through Business* (Montrose: Manna Ventures, 1995), 113; and David Bussau and Russell Mask, *Christian Microenterprise Development: An Introduction* (Oxford: Regnum Books, 2003), 11.

16. David J. Bosch, *Transforming Mission: Paradigm Shifts in Theology of Mission* (New York: Orbis, 2008), 341.

17. Bussau and Mask, *Christian Microenterprise Development*.

lack of proclamation. In such instances microfinance becomes merely a social action activity which may be very helpful as a development project given that the microfinance activities are structured in such a form that they do produce a social good. At the same time, however, they may be relatively unrelated to the proclamation of the gospel, a vital component in integral mission theology. Some Christian microfinance organizations are becoming acutely aware of the seriousness of the issue.[18]

It is thus increasingly important to define biblical boundaries for the use of microfinance as a form of social action in Christian mission. In principle this is not limited to microfinance, but extends to any form of integral mission activity. The need to maintain the proclamation of the gospel in some form and defining how this may be done is additionally important because microfinance absorbs a lot of capital and human resources in Christian mission work.

Some might argue that there is no substantial difference between social action and evangelism, that they are not distinct activities. Reference is sometimes made to the statement said to originate with St Francis of Assisi that "we should preach always, sometimes using words,"[19] thus downplaying the need to maintain proclamation as a necessary part of Christian mission. However, it may also be argued that without communication "social action is like a signpost pointing nowhere, and may be even in the wrong direction, to ourselves and our own charitable acts."[20]

The biblical perspectives on social action as an element in integral mission activities like microfinance are thus important when considering the use of this vehicle in the work of Christian missions. It is therefore important to clarify what the integral mission concept in mainstream evangelical thinking implies and what it requires of churches and Christian NGOs. As many Christian agencies, NGOs and missions have incorporated microfinance in their strategies for social action with a focus on overcoming poverty and exclusion, and more are in the process of moving into microfinance, it is important that a clearer picture of tendencies toward "mission drift" in the microfinance activities of Christian mission is established. Only thus may shortcomings be rectified and deviations from a biblical mission platform be removed.

---

18. For example, Bussau and Mask, *Christian Microenterprise Development*, 67.

19. St Francis of Assisi as referred to by Tim Chester, *Good News to the Poor* (Nottingham: IVP, 2004), 65.

20. Chester, *Good News*, 65.

The following chapters will deal with these issues as follows:

Chapter 2, "A Theological Perspective," explores the development of the integral mission concept and to what extent the evangelical community has come to a theological consensus on the role of proclamation in Christian social action. The understanding of Christian integral mission as adopted and clarified through the Lausanne process as the evangelical platform for mission has been chosen as a basis for an appraisal of microfinance in Christian mission. The reason for this choice is that the Lausanne process constitutes the broadest and most inclusive evangelical platform for thinking on the relationship between evangelism and social action. The initiation of the process was characterized by *Time* Magazine as "possibly the widest ranging meeting of Christians ever held,"[21] and there have been consultations on key topics at regular intervals. The most recent consultation in the context of what is officially called the Lausanne Congress on World Evangelization was held in Cape Town in South Africa in October 2010, gathering thousands of evangelical leaders from all over the world.

The origins and the development of the integral mission concept are important as they may partly explain some of the reasons for problems encountered in its application in ongoing Christian social action operations. Finally, the chapter explores the criteria by which the operations of Christian microfinance may be assessed with respect to meeting the material and the spiritual needs of the poor, and which in turn may facilitate identification of "mission drift."

Chapter 3, "Microfinance in Christian Mission and Perceived Effects on the Poor," is an assessment of the performance of Christian microfinance operations in relation to the challenge of delivering a social good to the poor and focuses on the role and performance of microfinance in Christian social action as a means to enable people to break out of the poverty cycle.[22] The chapter also discusses the specific challenges faced by Christian microfinance operations in relation to the proclamation part of Christian mission. The main reasons for mission drift in relation to the mandate to proclaim the gospel are explored, as well as the practical challenges related to maintaining proclamation in Christian microfinance activities. A main objective of the

---

21. *Time*, 5 August 1974, as quoted by Timothy Dudley-Smith, *John Stott: A Global Ministry* (Leicester: Inter-Varsity Press, 2001), 209.

22. Social action activities are programs which express the concern of God for justice and reconciliation throughout human society and for the liberation of human beings from every kind of oppression.

chapter is to establish a basis for an empirical study to appraise the potential of Christian microfinance as a vehicle in Christian integral mission.

Chapter 4 is a field study in the Philippine and Thai microfinance industries to test the assumption that it is possible to have a financially sustainable microfinance operation that can deliver a social good to the poor at the same time as providing a bridge for the gospel. In other words the field study is an empirical test of whether microfinance can be a vehicle in integral mission. It is also a study of the risk factors or mechanisms that produce mission drift in relation to the objectives and requirements of integral mission theology. Ways to address the risk factors producing mission drift are illustrated by examples from microfinance in the Philippine and Thai Christian microfinance organizations.

By the end of this study I hope to have indicated some of the challenges to proclamation in microfinance in Christian mission, as well as some shortcomings and areas that might be strengthened or rectified.

The main contribution of the research may, however, be that some churches and Christian social action organizations are encouraged to rethink the way they operate so as to be able both to help people break out of poverty and social repression and to ensure that the proclamation part of the Great Commission of Christ has its rightful place.

2

A Theological Perspective

The main issue under consideration in this chapter is the nature of integral mission theology as understood in the context of the Lausanne process,[1] in particular whether or to what extent the proclamation of the gospel should be a part of a Christian social action operation for the activities performed to justify being called "integral Christian mission." I study the process leading to a concept of integral mission in the evangelical church and assess the effects of the perennial "priority of evangelism" debate about the relationship between social action and evangelism in integral mission. I introduce and discuss a new approach to solving the problems which are created by the lack of conceptual clarity. The concept of "mission drift" is introduced in relation to the broad consensus reached in the evangelical church that social action and evangelism are inextricably linked to each other. This consensus in turn forms the basis for the assessment of Christian microfinance as a vehicle for integral mission.

2.1 Brief Background to the Development of the Integral Mission Concept

As the introduction of the integral mission concept signalled a paradigm shift in mission thinking within the evangelical church worldwide, it was an event of major importance, and it may have far-reaching consequences. Below, the effects of the paradigm shift will be studied in relation to one area of social action that is pursued in the context of the integral mission concept: that of microfinance.

However, Christian social service operations appear in a number of areas, such as health, poverty abatement, and fighting social injustice; hence

---

1. The Lausanne process is described in section 2.2.2.

some conclusions drawn for social action programs to mitigate poverty in the world through microfinance may have parallels in other areas of social action. At the centre of this issue is the question of what is "mission" within the framework of the integrated mission concept as expressed in the many documents of evangelicalism since Lausanne 1974. In theological terms this discussion basically relates to the relationship between word and deed in the Christian faith. We shall ask to what extent there may be a general agreement among evangelicals on the necessity for a verbal proclamation of the gospel in the overall mission of the church. This warrants a study both of the conclusions in some of the key documents and of the declarations that underpin the widespread acceptance of the integrated mission concept and which seek to clarify it.

The significance of changing the concept of mission in evangelicalism may be highlighted by the quantitative growth of the evangelical church during the last forty years. The "conversionism" feature of evangelicalism may help to explain one of the major changes in the church that has been in progress in the twentieth century. This change has been a progress toward a world Christianity in which evangelical Christianity has an increasingly influential role.[2] The sheer magnitude of the change is illustrated by the increase in the number of evangelicals worldwide, from an estimated 277 million in 1970 to approximately 729 million today;[3] the evangelicals' relative share of world Christianity has increased from 22 percent (277 million out of 1,236 million) to 32 percent (729 million out of 2,245 million) during the same period.[4] These figures are naturally uncertain as they rest on the assumption that the registrations and classifications of evangelicals are correct. However, whatever the exact numbers are, there is little doubt that the evangelicals constitute a major and increasing part of the church in the world and that the evangelical movement is growing rapidly in Latin America, Asia and Africa, which in the period from 1970–2004 has increased from 19.43 million and 30 million to 62 and 129 million respectively.[5] Still McGrath maintains that evangelicalism

---

2. Peter Brierley, "Evangelicals in the World of the 21st Century," *2004 Forum on World Evangelization Program* (Lausanne: LCWE, 2004). A summary of the main features of evangelical Christianity may be found later in this section.

3. Ibid., table (7), 14.

4. Ibid., calculated on the basis of figures in table (4) and table (7), 9, 14.

5. Ibid., 14.

is "the slumbering giant in the world of spirituality."[6] He thereby indicates that numerical growth in church affiliation does not necessarily say much about the depth of evangelical spirituality – that is, the extent to which the individual Christians are committed to expressing the teaching of Christ in their own lives.

In spite of the great variety of practices and emphases among evangelicals there seems to be some agreement between scholars as to what constitutes the basic features of evangelical spirituality. The British historian D. Bebbington sees evangelical religion as comprising all evangelicals who have certain doctrines and practical emphases in common, the main ones being "conversionism," the belief that lives need to be changed; "activism," the expression of the gospel in the lives of believers; "biblicism," a high regard for the Bible; and finally, "crucicentrism," a stress on the sacrifice of Christ on the cross.[7] McGrath would agree with the features summarized by Bebbington, but would replace "activism" by the more narrow concept of "evangelism."

However, the growth in depth of evangelical spirituality is not easily measured. "Activism," "crucicentrism" and "biblicism" are not as readily quantifiable as "conversionism" as measured in terms of church affiliation. A concept of mission that in the past resulted in strong growth would not necessarily produce the same growth tomorrow.

It is in this context that we may understand the Lausanne process leading to a revised concept of Christian mission in evangelicalism. However, this process was not initiated by a concern over a lack of quantitative growth in the evangelical church, but rather, as we shall discuss in what follows, a growing concern about shallow discipleship: that the church was not true to Christ's call to mission in its entirety.

2.2 The Process toward a Concept of Integral Mission in Evangelical Theology

2.2.1 Definition of "Mission" and Early Tensions

Attempts to define "mission" seem to be of relatively recent date in the history of the church. David Bosch asserts that in the NT itself no such efforts are

6. A. E. McGrath, *Evangelicalism and the Future of Christianity* (London: Hodder & Stoughton, 1988), 142.

7. David W. Bebbington, *Evangelicalism in Modern Britain: A History from the 1730s to the 1980s* (London: Routledge, 1989).

made.[8] The same author argues that it is extraordinarily difficult to define "mission" and maintains that its definition is a "continual process of sifting, testing, reformulating and discarding."[9] One may not agree that the mission concept in the NT suffers from this lack of clarity; at the same time it seems likely that the way mission is understood by a church or a Christian NGO will impact the practical mission behaviour in a wide range of activities, such as health and education, teaching, and social action areas like working for justice and peace, poverty alleviation, welfare, non-violence and reconciliation. All this is carried out to reflect what is perceived as a hallmark of mission: love of human beings reflected in an effort to meet both their spiritual and human needs.[10] A more defined concept of Christian mission is provided by Christopher J. H. Wright, who affirms that at the centre of any biblically based theology of mission must be the cross of Christ, as the cross was the cost of God's mission, and "all mission flows from the cross."[11] He contends that an understanding of Christian mission must reflect the overall mission of God through history. He takes a somewhat different position from Bosch in relation to a biblical basis for mission when he says that there must be a "formal agreement between what the church does and what the biblical texts say."[12] On that basis he defines mission as "our committed participation as God's people, at God's invitation and command, in God's own mission within the history of God's world for the redemption of God's creation," and states categorically that "the Great Commission implies an imperative, a mandate."[13] In establishing his central thesis that mission is what "the Bible is all about"[14] and that "all mission flows from the cross" he argues that the cross must be as central to our social engagement as it is to our evangelism.[15]

An implicit tension between evangelism and social responsibility has prevailed since the beginning of modern mission history. The great revival in the UK and the US in the eighteenth century was characterized by both

8. Bosch, *Transforming Mission*, 511.

9. Ibid.

10. J. A. B. Jongeneel, "Mission Theology in the Twentieth Century," in John Corrie, *Dictionary of Mission Theology: Evangelical Foundations* (Downers Grove: IVP, 2007), 142.

11. Christopher J. H. Wright, *The Mission of God: Unlocking the Bible's Grand Narrative* (Downers Grove: IVP, 2006), 312, 314.

12. Ibid., 36.

13. Ibid., 51.

14. Ibid., 29.

15. Ibid., 315.

evangelism and a concern for the poor. In North America Jonathan Edwards considered God's work of redemption to be reflected both in the conversion and sanctification of individuals and in God's grand design in creation, history and providence.[16] These aspects of God's work were considered inseparable. In his thinking the church had two mandates, proclamation and practical social action. In the Evangelical Awakening in the UK the enthusiasm for revival led to a broader social commitment to reform for the benefit of the poor.[17]

However, after a while the evangelical churches in both countries moved away from this two-pronged understanding of the task of the church. One important contributing factor was the rise of the social gospel movement that put the emphasis of the gospel on the present era. The movement was theologically underpinned by Walter Rauschenbusch, the author of *Christianity and the Social Order* (1912) and *A Theology for the Social Gospel* (1917). The new gospel of the kingdom of God was the struggle over time to move toward a Christian society in which social life would be a reflection of true Christian values. This he contrasted with the old gospel of saving souls.

The evangelical reaction to the social gospel movement was to move away altogether from maintaining two separate but interlinked mandates, the one of proclaiming the gospel and the other of working for social justice. By the early twentieth century many evangelicals rejected outright social involvement as a part of the mission of the church.[18] Evangelism was not only gradually given primacy in the mission of the church, but evangelism alone was mission. Between 1900 and 1930 progressive social mission concerns tended to disappear from the evangelical movement.[19] At that time the evangelical movement was termed "fundamentalist" as it wanted to preserve the fundamentals of the gospel.[20]

Gradually this narrow understanding of the mission of the church came under pressure. Most evangelical churches and mission agencies in the first seventy years of the twentieth century tended to apply the narrow definition of mission with an emphasis on proclamation as the key component of Christian mission (e.g. Matt 28:19). However, this does not mean that

---

16. Bosch, *Transforming Mission*, 403.
17. Ibid.
18. Chester, *Good News*, 74.
19. Bosch, *Transforming Mission*, 404.
20. J. I. Packer, *"Fundamentalism" and the Word of God* (London: IVP, 1965), 24.

Christian missions during the first seventy years of the twentieth century did not also often include many humanitarian elements. Christian missionaries were not exclusively preoccupied with "saving souls." Schools and hospitals, orphanages, and so on, were established in all parts of the world. But these humanitarian and social components in the mission work were not a part of their strict definition of the mission mandate although they tended to be an integral part of the practical mission work itself.

A change in the view of mainstream evangelical churches was visible after the Second World War. One of the protagonists was the conservative theologian Carl Henry, whose book *The Uneasy Conscience of Modern Fundamentalism*, published in 1947, became catalytic; he concluded that "there is no room . . . for gospel that is indifferent to the needs of the total man, or of the global man."[21] Also the *missio Dei* concept – that the Father, Son and Holy Spirit are sending the church into the world – impacted mission thinking in the post-war period.[22] The understanding that the core meaning of *missio Dei* is that mission is the mission of the triune God influences evangelical theologians even up to the present day. "God is on mission, and we . . . are co-workers with God (1 Cor 3:9)."[23]

The process of redefining or reinterpreting the relationship between evangelism and social concerns led to renewed discussions at a number of larger conferences. The Wheaton Declaration in 1966 stated that social concerns were important, but without minimizing the priority of preaching the gospel.[24] The Berlin Congress in 1966 affirmed the dedication of the church to the task of evangelizing the world for Christ while at the same time including a social dimension within evangelism.[25]

---

21. Cited in Bosch, *Transforming Mission*, 404.

22. Bosch, *Transforming Mission*, 390.

23. Wright, *The Mission of God*, 531.

24. "The Wheaton Declaration," Billy Graham Center Archives, http://www.wheaton.edu/bgc/archives/docs/wd66/b08.html; accessed 10 November 2010.

25. The World Congress on Evangelism, Berlin, 25 October – 1 November 1966, was initiated by American Protestant leaders to provide a forum for a growing evangelical Protestant movement worldwide and intended as a special successor to the 1910 World Missionary Conference in Edinburgh, Scotland. The Congress was financed with support from the Billy Graham Evangelistic Association and *Christianity Today*. There were 1,200 invited delegates. Christian social responsibility was summarized in Article 5 in the Covenant.

2.2.2 The International Congress on World Evangelization (ICOWE) in 1974

This interpretation of the relationship between evangelism and social responsibility came under increasing criticism which culminated with the International Congress on World Evangelization (ICOWE) in Lausanne in 1974, a turning point in the modern theology of mission.

One of the stated objectives of the proceedings of the Lausanne Congress was to re-emphasize those aspects which are essential to evangelism. There were two aspects of a more operational nature: "Christian witness by both word and deed" (neither denying social responsibility nor making it "our all-consuming mission," and "the necessity of evangelism for the salvation of souls"). This was underlined in the introductory address in which Billy Graham stated that his personal hope "was that the Congress would state what the relationship is between evangelism and social responsibility."[26] In principle the Congress was successful in achieving a broad-based consensus among the participants, as the Lausanne Covenant reads: "Evangelism and socio-political involvement are both part of our Christian duty. For both are necessary expressions of our doctrines of God and man, our love for our neighbour and our obedience to Jesus Christ."[27]

However, the Lausanne Congress did not manage to clarify how evangelism and socio-political involvement should relate to each other more specifically, although the Covenant states that evangelism is primary – "In the Church's sacrificial service evangelism is primary"[28] – and that "although reconciliation with man is not reconciliation with God, nor is social action evangelism, nor is political liberation salvation, nevertheless we affirm that evangelism and socio-political involvement are both part of our Christian duty . . . and faith without works is dead."[29]

The explicit statement that social action is not evangelism is of significance as it gave at least an overall guidance to churches and mission groups of all kinds by implying that social action should contain an element of evangelism.

In the aftermath of the Congress the Lausanne Covenant was considered unclear by many as it did not spell out in detail how evangelism and social

---

26. Billy Graham, as cited in Stott, *Making Christ Known*, 4.
27. The Lausanne Covenant, section 5, as cited in Stott, *Making Christ Known*, 24.
28. Stott, *Making Christ Known*, xix.
29. Ibid., 24.

responsibility related to each other in real-life situations.[30] The critics were both those who demanded a return to the old concept of mission based on evangelism only, and those who felt that the Lausanne Congress, by giving priority to evangelism in the integrated mission mandate, had not gone far enough toward making evangelism and social action equal activities.

2.2.3 The Grand Rapids Consultation

As the relationship between evangelism and social responsibility was not resolved at the Lausanne Congress efforts were made later to clarify the issue. In the following years a number of conferences were arranged that occasionally touched on the issue. However, the International Consultation on the Relationship between Evangelism and Social Responsibility (CRESR) that was sponsored by the Lausanne Committee for World Evangelism and the World Evangelical Fellowship at Grand Rapids Springs, Michigan, 19–25 June 1982, focused entirely on it. However, the preamble to the report written by the chairman of the consultation, John Stott, conveyed the lack of convictions about the possibility of reaching a conclusion as to the exact relationship between evangelism and social responsibility when he wrote that the pre-eminence given to evangelism in integral mission in the Lausanne statement was accepted for the sake of maintaining the partnership.[31]

The Grand Rapids Consultation did not reach any final conclusions, but some clarifications were made.

First the report states clearly that the Bible distinguishes between evangelism and social responsibility. In other words, they are different activities but "At the same time they belong to each other."[32] This statement is a reflection of the Lausanne formulation about evangelism and socio-political involvement (section 5) that they are both part of our Christian duty.

---

30. E.g. Arthur Johnston, *The Battle for World Evangelism*, criticizes the Lausanne movement, first, for going the same way as the World Council of Churches, and second, for going soft on the Bible and evangelism. Finally he refers to John Stott as "having de-throned" evangelism as the traditional and primary task of the church. Cited in Dudley-Smith, *John Stott*, 303.

31. The partnership referred to is the partnership between evangelicals of different persuasions belonging to the Lausanne movement. Stott, *Making Christ Known*, 170.

32. Lausanne Occasional Paper (LOP) 21, "Evangelism and Social Responsibility: An Evangelical Commitment," joint publication of the Lausanne Committee for World Evangelization (LCWE) and the World Evangelical Fellowship (WEF), Lausanne Movement, 1982, section A; http://www.lausanne.org/content/lop/lop-21; accessed 10 January 2010.

Another important clarification of the consultation was to emphasize that, although evangelism and social responsibility belong to each other, this does not necessarily imply that they can never exist independently of each other.[33] There are a number of instances in the NT where it was legitimate to pursue one without the other.[34] Neither is it illegitimate to have an evangelistic campaign without a program for social service.[35] The conclusions of the report thus seem to imply an agreement between the participants that there is no biblical basis to maintain that evangelism and social action should follow exactly the same chronological order. As to how evangelism and social responsibility *in general* relate to each other the report describes them in terms of four relationships which carry importance for integral mission and social action programs as they all relate to the chronological relationship between them *over a time horizon.*

The first is that social activity is a *consequence* of evangelism, as new Christians that are actively encouraged to get involved in serving others will strengthen social service to meet local human needs.[36]

Second, the report says that social responsibility is one of the *principal aims* of evangelism, referring to Ephesians 2:10: "we are created in Christ Jesus for good works which God prepared beforehand, that we should walk in them." Although there is no automatic cause and effect relationship between faith and good deeds the report argues that the church has a responsibility to include this relationship in its ministry.

The report also argues that social activity may be a *bridge* to evangelism as it breaks down prejudice and suspicion, thereby opening closed doors and opening the minds of people to the gospel.[37] A number of examples are cited that demonstrate this aspect of social service endeavours.

Lastly the consultation states that social activity may also be a *partner* in evangelism. For many Christian missions this partnership between evangelism and social service constitutes the historical basis for their operations.[38] The report argues that Christian action may be "not bribes, but bridges of love

---

33. Ibid., section B.

34. Stott, *Making Christ Known*, 180.

35. LOP 21, 7, section B.

36. Ibid., section C.

37. Ibid., 8, section C.

38. An example of this is the Norwegian Mission Alliance which since 1905 has been committed to integral mission with its motto "The Word and Deed, hand in hand" (translated from Norwegian).

to the world," as in the life of Jesus Christ the *kerygma* (proclamation) and *diakonia* (service) went hand-in-hand. He proclaimed the gospel of the kingdom and healed the sick, his words explaining his actions and his actions his words.[39]

In addition to the above clarifications on the *general* relationship between social action and evangelism, the consultation also made an attempt to clarify the various forms in which social concerns have been expressed in the church. Keeping in mind the focus in this paper on microfinance it is useful to note that with respect to development efforts made by the church the consultation stressed a need for sustainability in the form of self-help programs so as not to reinforce dependence.[40]

However, the report is quite clear that evangelism and social action "should not be identified with each other, for evangelism is not social responsibility, nor is social responsibility evangelism. Yet each involves the other."[41] This is an important clarifying statement, but a mandate which is so general can hardly be said to be an adequate guide when it comes to the practical structuring of strategies for Christian mission operation. Maybe it was the awareness of this that led the participants of the consultation into an attempt to debate the question of primacy.

The Grand Rapids Consultation gave primacy to evangelism by affirming the Lausanne Covenant statement that "In the Church's mission of sacrificial service evangelism is primary" (paragraph 6). But the clarification did not really confer any practical operational benefit for missions as the nearly 20,000-word report goes on to say that "we are not referring to an invariable temporal priority, because in some situations a social ministry will take precedence, but to a logical one . . . the reason being that social activity is a consequence and aim of evangelism (as we have asserted), then evangelism must precede it."[42] Furthermore, people's eternal destiny is related to their hearing and receiving the gospel, thus in a situation of choice, "a person's eternal, spiritual salvation is of greater importance than his or her temporal needs and material well-being."[43] The consultation did not go much further, other than stating that the choice between the two is rather theoretical as they

---

39. LOP 21, 8, section C.
40. Stott, *Making Christ Known*, 197.
41. Ibid., 182.
42. Ibid., 183.
43. Ibid.

are inseparable, as in the public ministry of Jesus, and not competing with each other. But rather, the consultation continues, they mutually support and strengthen each other "in an upward spiral of increased concern for both."[44]

Thus CRESR in principle upheld the main conclusions of the Lausanne Congress. The intricate four-dimensional relationship between evangelism and social responsibility as discussed above was illustrated by various examples underlining the difficulty of deriving any practical guidelines for mission operations from the Grand Rapids Consultation. The official evangelical position was then, and still is, that Christian mission consists of two legs, evangelism and social action, and that they should be inextricably linked, not one without the other; and that the primacy of evangelism is to be maintained.

2.2.4 The Priority of Evangelism in Integral Mission Thinking: A Dichotomy?

Although the Lausanne Congress and the Grand Rapids Consultation were able to find a compromise on formulations regarding the relationship between evangelism and social action in integral mission, there have been undercurrents of disagreement on some key issues, particularly the priority given to evangelism in mission, but also regarding the idea that the integral mission concept contains two components, evangelism and social action, which are not identical.

The late D. Bosch contended that if mission is regarded as consisting of two separate components, this would be to concede that each of the two has a life of its own, and that it is thus possible to have evangelism without a social dimension, and Christian social involvement without an evangelistic dimension. He also argued that to afford primacy to evangelism is to imply that one is obligatory and the other optional.[45] It is difficult to see the strength in this argument as the opposite would be to imply that evangelism and social action are the same thing, which they quite clearly are not, although the relationship between them tends to be complex.

In a still deeper disagreement with the Lausanne Covenant Bosch maintained that CRESR upheld a dichotomy between mission and social responsibility primarily because the report gave the priority to proclamation when it stated that "in the Church's mission of sacrificial service evangelism

44. Ibid.
45. Bosch, *Transforming Mission*, 405.

is primary."[46] This may be an uncommon use of the term "dichotomy," and it may even be misleading to maintain that the Lausanne or the CRESR report upholds a dichotomy. Normally a dichotomy is understood to be a division into two sharply distinguished, opposed or contradictory parts or opinions. Proclamation and social action according to both Lausanne and the CRESR are parts of a whole, inextricably linked to each other. In general Christian mission should therefore consist of both activities.

Social action work, according to the final communiqué of the CRESR, originates from a conviction that social action is a result of faith in Christ and his proclamation of the kingdom. A dichotomy would exist if the alternative to proclamation was something entirely different.

Bosch also argued that the Lausanne Covenant contained a "dualism" by giving priority to evangelism. A dualism normally denotes two parts which are more or less independent of each other, the idea being that "for some particular domain there are two fundamental kinds or categories of things or principles."[47] It does not seem convincingly argued that the Lausanne statement and the subsequent Grand Rapids Consultation Report drive such a deep wedge between evangelism and social responsibility that a dualism has emerged. Instead it is explicitly stated in both declarations that the two components, social action and evangelism, are inextricably linked to each other in the integral mission concept and are profoundly interdependent, thus making up one single and unified mission concept.

There may, however, have been a trend toward a weakening of the priority of evangelism in integrated mission thinking after Grand Rapids. A World Evangelical Fellowship (WEF) consultation in Wheaton in 1983 may exemplify this trend as the conference did not give any priority to evangelism, nor was there an affirmation of an inextricable link between social action and evangelism in its final statement: "The mission of the church includes both the proclamation of the Gospel and its demonstration. We must therefore evangelize, respond to immediate human needs and press for social transformation."[48] Thus there was still some dissatisfaction in the evangelical community that the priority of evangelism had been maintained in the Lausanne mandate.

---

46. Ibid., 406, referring to section 6 in the Lausanne Covenant.
47. Howard Robinson, "Dualism," Stanford Encyclopedia of Philosophy, rev. 3 November 2011, http://plato.stanford.edu/contents.html; accessed on 15 January 2010.
48. Bosch, Transforming Mission, 407.

In the mind of critics of the Lausanne Covenant and the Grand Rapids Consultation, such as David Bosch, the Wheaton statement did not contain the previously described perennial dichotomy as the priority given to evangelism was removed.[49] Although the Wheaton statement does identify evangelism and social action/transformation as different activities it is also saying that both of them *are* mission. There is no attempt to respond to a need to maintain that evangelism and social action are integral and interlinked parts in a given mission effort, whether in a church context or an NGO social action type mission. It may be argued that this is a weakness in the Wheaton statement as evangelism is not integral mission on a stand-alone basis, and neither is social action. On their own, neither evangelism nor social action is integral mission.

The *raison d'être* for social action is the proclamation of Christ to love our neighbour as ourselves (Mark 12:31) and to help the poor and oppressed (Luke 4:18–19). Christ also stressed that those who follow him should not be ashamed of him (e.g. Luke 9:26). One may thus legitimately question the reluctance of Bosch to give the proclamation of Christ a primary position. The lack of clarity about the substance of integral mission which this reluctance results in may also be demonstrated by his definition of evangelism: "evangelism is that dimension and activity of the church's mission which by word and deed offers every person and community everywhere a valid opportunity to be directly challenged to a radical reorientation of their lives, a reorientation which involves such things as deliverance from slavery to the world and its powers; embracing Christ as Saviour and Lord . . ."[50] He does not say "deliverance from slavery" (and so on) "by embracing Christ as Saviour and Lord," but lets "deliverance from slavery to the world and its powers" remain entirely undefined, and he lets it precede "embracing Christ as Saviour and Lord." This leaves the reader with the idea that social action to improve the human condition is of equal importance as embracing Christ as Saviour and Lord, and that one may well be valid without the other.

In spite of the lack of consensus on the priority of evangelism within evangelicalism there has been a general consensus in major evangelical conferences and consultations that Christian mission requires a proclamation component. It may be maintained that there is "a strong consensus that mission involves evangelism to proclaim the good news and social action to

---

49. Ibid.
50. Ibid., 420.

embody it."[51] Attempts to equate evangelism with social action could lead to lack of clarity in the concept of Christian mission and the Great Commission. It may be this lack of clarity of direction in mission that Bishop O'Neill has in mind when he says, "If everything is mission, nothing is mission."[52]

2.2.5 The Manila Manifesto and the Cape Town Commitment

In 1989, fifteen years after the Lausanne conference, the Second International Conference on World Evangelization, also called Lausanne II or Lausanne 89, was convened in Manila with more than 3,000 evangelical participants from 170 countries. The conference adopted the "Manila Manifesto" to form the basis for further study and response. Six principal affirmations were made that pertain to the topic under discussion, the balance between social responsibility and evangelism. Affirmation 16 restated the evangelistic and social action duty as "every Christian congregation must turn itself outward to its local community in evangelistic witness and compassionate love." In Affirmation 18 followed the pledge to develop a strategy to ensure that the church can function in the way envisaged: "We affirm our duty to study the society in which we live, to understand its structures, values and needs, and so develop an appropriate strategy for mission."[53]

The integrated mission concept was thus affirmed in unequivocal terms. In the words of the chairperson the Manila Manifesto was primarily a renewed call for "the whole church to take the whole gospel to the whole world."[54] Thus the Manila conference did not change the stance taken by the evangelical community on the relationship between evangelism and social responsibility at the Grand Rapids Conference. But neither did the Manila conference improve on the Grand Rapids discussions' inability to come up with more practical guidelines to the church with respect to the balance between social responsibility and evangelism.

The Third Lausanne Congress on World Evangelism, also called Lausanne III, was held in Cape Town, South Africa, in October 2010. The Congress did not attempt to bring any more clarity as to the balance between social responsibility and evangelism, but maintained that "evangelism is the

---

51. Nigel Wright, *The Radical Evangelical* (London: SPCK, 1996), 106.

52. Stephen Neill, *Creative Tension* (London: Edinburgh House Press, 1959), 81.

53. Lausanne Movement, "Manila Manifesto," http://www.lausanne.org/content/manifesto/the-manila-manifesto; accessed 6 May 2011.

54. Dudley-Smith, *John Stott*, 303.

proclamation of the historical biblical Christ as Lord and Saviour . . . integral mission is the proclamation and demonstration of the gospel," and "It is not simply that evangelism and social involvement are to be done alongside each other," but that "our proclamation has social consequences."[55]

2.2.6 Further Work on the Link between Social Responsibility and Evangelism

An indication that the Lausanne movement continues to seek clarification with respect to the relationship between proclamation and social action may be found in the works of Christopher Wright, the chair of the Lausanne movement's Theology Working Group. In his book *The Mission of God* he seeks to bring the discussion forward by proposing the replacement of the term "priority" or "primacy" of evangelism in mission with the concept of "ultimacy" of evangelism in mission.[56] By introducing the idea of "ultimacy" of evangelism he wants to signal that in a local context with a great variety of human and social needs which might require a social action response as well as proclamation of the gospel, the church must "ultimately" not be satisfied until the good news of Christ has been proclaimed. Hence although mission may not always have evangelism as the starting point, he contends that without proclamation of the gospel the mission is defective, and it will not be holistic mission. Care is needed in engaging with Wright on this issue. He is not against "primacy" of evangelism in principle as he reflects the Grand Rapids Report by maintaining that there is a strong logic for primacy of evangelism in that "Christian social action (as part of mission) requires the existence of socially active Christians. And as that presupposes the evangelism by which they came to faith in Christ" this gives evangelism a "kind of chronological as well as theological primacy."[57] However, he levels a complaint against the stance taken in the Lausanne process in that he is critical of the use of the words "primacy" or "priority" with regard to evangelism in mission and is searching for a more suitable concept to replace them. Wright contends that "priority" implies that everything else is "secondary," and furthermore that "priority" implies that evangelism also has to be the starting point. Some of this reasoning is reminiscent of the line of argument pursued by Bosch, who

---

55. Lausanne Movement, "The Cape Town Commitment: A Declaration of Belief and Call to Action," 24 October 2010, Part I, Section C.

56. Wright, *The Mission of God*, 316.

57. Ibid., 318.

contended that if one aspect (i.e. evangelism) is obligatory, everything else is optional.[58]

Wright's second proposal is that proclamation should be viewed in the context of a local community, thus reflecting Affirmation 16 in the Manila Manifesto. This is a practical approach to integral mission, as situations in which social action could be viewed as, for example, a "bridge to evangelism" would naturally tend to occur in a local context.

It is not difficult to agree with Wright that if "priority" means that everything else is "secondary," then the concept of "priority" would be misplaced. Holistic mission is based on the concept of the wholeness of human beings. However, his critique of the use of "priority" of mission is problematic on a number of levels.

First, in order to clarify the reason for his position Wright refers to the enumeration of Paul in Romans 13 of the various ministries in the church to show that Christians have different callings and that nothing is secondary.[59] But he would still agree that all Christians should be witnesses "whatever the context of work."[60] Thus he seems to agree that proclamation is not necessarily preaching; it may simply mean "sharing the message of the gospel with people on a personal level."[61] The same is expressed in the Lausanne Covenant that simply states that evangelism is "the proclamation of Christ with a view to persuading people to come to him personally and so be reconciled to God."[62]

Second, the word "priority" in connection with evangelism may not necessarily imply that it is the unique starting point. An alternative understanding of "priority" may be drawn from a definition in the US military dictionary: "Priority might be an indication of importance so that you never leave it out, rather than an exclusive and first designation of the order of accomplishment."[63] Hence "priority" may also be understood as something that in general should never be left undone at any time in Christian mission. It may mean that whatever is done, it should also be ensured that the gospel is shared in the local mission context, at least on the personal level. However, evangelism in the form of a more institutionalized activity

---

58. Bosch, *Transforming Mission*, 407.

59. Wright, *The Mission of God*, 322.

60. Ibid.

61. Chester, *Good News*, 56.

62. Stott, *Making Christ Known*, 22.

63. "Priority," US Military Dictionary, at Answers, http://www.answers.com/topic/priority, accessed 15 March 2010.

(campaigns of various kinds, public preaching, etc.) would in certain specific cultural situations have to be adapted to an overall integral mission strategy in a planned fashion along a timescale, where social action might be a bridge to more broad-based evangelism at a later stage.

Third, Wright contends that holistic mission is the responsibility of the whole church and not of any one individual.[64] Few would dispute this statement. However, it is problematic in that he may give the impression that a Christian social action group might leave all responsibility for evangelism to the church at large, assuming that ultimately someone will take care of it. A logical response to a general statement of the need for "ultimacy" might be to say that where there is no specific assignment of responsibility for evangelism, there is no one responsible for its being accomplished. Wright also stops short of saying that every mission in a local context should have a strategic plan along a timescale that includes the "ultimacy" of evangelism. It may thus be argued that the use of the word "ultimacy" may ultimately be counterproductive to evangelism if it has no timeframe. Without a timeframe, "ultimacy" of evangelism refers to an event that may hopefully take place in the short, medium or long term. "Ultimacy" thus simply implies that at some point in the future someone should take care of evangelism. It reminds us a bit of Maynard Keynes, the well-known economist, who in a famous remark stressed that "the long run" is a misleading guide to current affairs, as "in the long run we are all dead."[65]

What would be the implications of Wright's input in the "primacy" debate? The idea of "ultimacy" of evangelism could be useful as a guiding tool if it could also imply that integral mission is viewed in a local context, and if the planned evangelism is a part of an overall integral mission strategy for activities along a timescale. A broadened ultimacy of evangelism concept might also provide the church with a better clarification of the relationship between proclamation and evangelism in integral mission. Thus the ultimacy of evangelism concept would appear to have the potential to give effective guidance to the church, and in particular to the operators of social action programs in Christian mission. For this to be realized it would be required not only that "ultimacy" of evangelism is viewed in a local context, but also that evangelism is part and parcel of an overall strategic plan that will be

---

64. Wright, *The Mission of God*, 322.

65. John Maynard Keynes, cited by John Sloman, "How to Kick-Start a Faltering Economy the Keynes Way," BBC News Magazine, 22 October 2008, http://news.bbc.co.uk/2/hi/uk_news/magazine/7682887.stm.

implemented along a timescale in a church-based or NGO-based Christian mission program.

Once the ultimacy of evangelism concept is applied in this way it may be argued that there is very little difference between this concept and the concept of the "primacy" of evangelism, given that the latter is defined as something that should never be left undone. However, one reason for maintaining the use of the word "priority" of evangelism might simply be that deep spiritual needs will always exist, whereas the extent, structure and content of other human and social needs at the level either of the individual or of society are not a priori definable as they tend to vary greatly from one social situation and country to another.

Wright embraces a conclusion from an article by Paul Heldt that describes two extreme views to avoid: proclamation only, or social action only. "Both approaches are unbiblical"; "Mission is, by definition, 'holistic,' and therefore 'holistic mission' is, de facto, mission."[66] This tautology may not be helpful in the future shaping of Christian integral mission. The discussion of the balance between evangelism and social action will most likely continue until the necessity for proclamation is expressed as incumbent on every Christian social action program in the context of their planned activities along a timescale, whether in the context of the "ultimacy" or the "primacy" of evangelism.

2.3 Issues Related to Proclamation in Integral Mission

2.3.1 Meaning of Proclamation

As evangelism and social action are intrinsically linked to each other in the integral mission concept it is legitimate to evaluate the meaning of proclamation, and in particular how explicit proclamation should be in various settings, cultures, political systems, and so on.

Proclamation is essentially the communication of the gospel message, the mystery of salvation realized for all in Jesus Christ. Implicit in proclamation is an invitation to commitment of faith in Jesus Christ and entry into the fellowship of believers. However, proclamation may happen in private conversations (e.g. Acts 8:30–38) as well as in a public places (e.g. Acts 2:14–

---

66. Jean-Paul Heldt, "Revisiting the Whole Gospel: Towards a Biblical Model of Holistic Mission in the 21st Century," *Missiology* 32 (2004): 149–72; cited by Wright, *The Mission of God*, 323.

42). The church is called to proclaim without hesitation that Christ is the way, the truth and the life (e.g. Rom 1:8).

In a sense it may be said that proclamation constitutes the basis for evangelism, which is related more specifically to the act of spreading the gospel message. Proclamation is thus a somewhat broader term than evangelism, which is an NT term derived from *euangelizein* and *euangelion*.[67] However, the two terms have tended to be translated "preach the gospel" and "the gospel" respectively.[68] In the Lausanne Covenant evangelism is spreading the good news of the gospel, which involves a proclamation of the historical, biblical Christ as Saviour and Lord. The main difference between proclamation and evangelism is that evangelism, in addition to being a verbal proclamation of the gospel, is normally used to refer to the activities involved in spreading the gospel with the specific aim of bringing people to faith in Christ, incorporation in the church and responsible service.[69]

Central to proclamation and evangelism in the integral mission concept is the meaning of the statement of Christ "that repentance and forgiveness of sins should be preached in his name to all nations" (Luke 24:47). The apostle Paul indicated the significance of making the gospel known when he exclaimed, "Woe to me if I do not preach the gospel" (1 Cor 9:16). Paul also indicated that the gospel preached by him was a concept clearly understood by his listeners when he said that there is no other gospel: "But even if we, or an angel from heaven, should preach to you a gospel contrary to that which we preached to you, let him be accursed" (Gal 1:8). In the Gospels Jesus is presented as the Messiah who fulfilled the prophecies, the arrival of a new event: the advent of a new era, the coming of the kingdom of God. The announcement in the Gospels is "that God intervenes in human history through the person and work of His Son."[70] The apostolic mission is rooted in the life of Christ and the Great Commission to bring salvation to all nations. Hence the gospel has a clear soteriological content as salvation is liberation from the consequences of sin (John 3:17), liberation from the power of sin (Rom 5:17; Col 3:3–4), and a complete restoration of humanity to the image

---

67. Barclay M. Newman, Jr., *A Concise Greek–English Dictionary of the New Testament* (Stuttgart: Deutsche Bibelgesellschaft, 1993), 75.

68. Bosch, *Transforming Mission*, 409.

69. Stott, *Making Christ Known*, 21.

70. C. René Padilla, *Misión integral: Ensayos sobre el Reino y la Iglesia* (Spanish edn; Grand Rapids: Eerdmans, 1986), 71. Quotation translated from the Spanish.

of God.[71] The preaching of the gospel contains elements which run through all of the NT: the call to repent, receive forgiveness of sins and believe (Mark 1:4; Luke 3:3). This is perhaps most clearly spelled out in the statement by Christ: "And that repentance and forgiveness of sins should be preached to all nations, beginning from Jerusalem" (Luke 24:47).

Another aspect of the gospel which runs through the NT is the link between faith and life. When Paul states that "we are his workmanship, created in Christ Jesus for good works, which God has prepared beforehand, that we should walk in them" (Eph 2:10), this reflects the teaching of Christ throughout his ministry that his followers should "love one another, as I have loved you" (John 15:12) and should teach new disciples to observe "all that I have commanded you" (Matt 28:20).

Proclamation and evangelism are hence at the core of Christian mission; they constitute a unique and sacred duty incumbent upon the church and thus are not an optional extra.[72] The priority given to evangelism in the Lausanne statement as well as at Grand Rapids, and affirmed by the Manila conference, implies that there is no mission without evangelism, and this forms the basis for the general theological stance in evangelicalism on the relationship between social responsibility and evangelism.

2.3.2 The Challenge of Mission Drift

A negation of a distinction between evangelism and social action may have some immediate consequences. The effect of a negation is described by one writer when he says that those who do not make this distinction thereby "conflate social action and proclamation into one activity . . . the ensuing problem is that this usually ends up with one aspect – and it is usually evangelism, being lost"; he concludes, "We must not do social action without evangelism."[73] In other words, social action should somehow be linked to a call to repentance and faith, and he is concerned that this is not always done.[74] Hence the prevailing concern about mission drift is not unfounded. The concept of mission drift is not something new as many initiatives based on the Christian faith have gradually steered away from their initial mission

---

71. Ibid., 77.
72. Bosch, *Transforming Mission*, 415.
73. Chester, *Good News*, 64–65.
74. C. René Padilla, *Mission Between the Times* (Grand Rapids: Eerdmans, 1985), 66.

objective and become unrecognizable when compared with their original mission.[75] One important reason for that may be the trend toward equating proclamation with social service.

When there is a lack of balance between these two legs of integrated mission the inevitable result may correctly be called "mission drift." A mission drift may occur even in movements where the integral mission theology is in line with the broad stance on mission in evangelicalism, but a number of factors both within the movement and from the outside weaken the proclamation part of the social action program. This issue will be discussed in chapter 3.

Although mission theology in the post-war period was in the process of being reformulated (see above under 2.2.1 and *missio Dei*) it may be argued that prior to Lausanne in the twentieth century evangelical mission theology and practice were primarily based on the understanding that the task to be undertaken by the church of God was to preach the gospel of salvation for the conversion of individuals. The concept of integral mission is, on the other hand, less clear cut and requires much work at the implementation stage in practical mission work.

If there should be a general trend in parts of the evangelical community toward an understanding of Christian mission in which social action programs may be defended as Christian mission on a stand-alone basis without proclamation, this might indeed be called a paradigm change of Christian mission. Such a change would probably be larger than the change in the early twentieth century to the one-mandate mission concept to evangelize, a one-mandate mission which is now fading and which it took much effort to change.[76] Thus the development of the integral mission theology, however important and justified it may be, tends to leave the church with the downside possibility that proclamation is weakened as the church gets involved in the wide range of options for social action with limited operational guidance as to how to make sure that the words of Christ "to make disciples of all nations" are accomplished in a social action context.

This lack of clarity on how to implement the concept of integral mission may be an explanatory factor as to why proclamation of the gospel may gradually be weakened in those parts of Christian social action where high

---

75. Peter Greer and Phil Smith, *The Poor Will Be Glad: Joining the Revolution to Lift the World Out of Poverty* (Grand Rapids: Zondervan, 2009), 195.
76. David Smith, *Mission After Christendom* (London: Darton, Longman & Todd, 2003), 7.

degrees of specialization and professional focus are a requirement for success. Hence, even though the theology of mission may be soundly based on an integral mission concept, in the course of time, because of professional and cultural pressures of various kinds, the strength of proclamation may slowly be impaired.

In the integral mission theology as defined by the evangelical community in the course of the Lausanne process evangelism and social responsibility are neither equal activities, nor do they have the same impact. The Lausanne process, by giving primacy to proclamation, established that the clearest defined need of the poor is to be reconciled to God. Social services, although valuable and able to demonstrate the gospel, may be like a signpost with no direction if there is no proclamation.[77] There is even a risk that by doing only good works we point to ourselves and not to Jesus Christ, and we may convey the idea that economic and social development is the most important aspect of human life.[78] Social services and evangelism are intricately linked in the documents of the Lausanne process and social action should therefore have an element of proclamation of the gospel.

Hence, if proclamation tends not to be incorporated explicitly in Christian service work, it is legitimate to ask both why that is so, and how that may be rectified in such a way that proclamation becomes an integral part of mission work. As in the context of the Lausanne process nothing is mission without proclamation, it is warranted to pay more attention to the issue of how to preserve this aspect of integral mission.

2.3.3 Form and Extent of Proclamation

As proclamation is central to mission there is a need to be explicit as to what proclamation entails in various contexts. Some work has been done to clarify this issue, such as in the context of the Grand Rapids Consultations (2.2.3 above). And yet it is crucial that this is clarified in order for us to have an integrated mission concept that is operational in particular mission situations. One author argues that none of the texts in the NT on the kingdom of God or the coming of the kingdom of God via societal change are without a confession of Christ.[79] However, in order to ensure that contextualized

---

77. Chester, *Good News*, 65.

78. Ibid.

79. Ronald Sider with James Parker, "How Broad Is Salvation in Scripture?" in *In Word and Deed*, ed. Bruce Nicholls (Carlisle: Paternoster, 1985), 104.

proclamation becomes a normal part of social action programs, there is a need in the church to study mechanisms that can ensure that a balance is maintained between proclamation and the specific Christian social action programs. Some evangelical theologians have been quite explicit with respect to the requirement that Christian mission activities of any kind should along the chronological timescale have a specific confession of Christ (see 2.2.3 above).

A clarification of this kind may enable Christian social action programs sponsored by churches or implemented by NGOs to reflect the proclamation mandate given by Christ in the Great Commission. The church is faced with a considerable challenge in relation to the task of preserving proclamation in church-based as well as NGO-operated social action activities.

Integral mission is multifaceted. The multiplicity of types of Christian social action programs in a great variety of cultures and subcultures implies that there is no single plan for integral mission which can be replicated everywhere. Each Christian integral mission program is itself responsible for designing how the inclusion of proclamation in its activities may be ensured.

One writer indicates that there is a need to make the evangelistic dimension of mission explicit: "It cannot be assumed that the evangelistic dimension of the church's mission is included in all that the church says and does."[80]

Thus the Lausanne process opened up conceptually to a complicated relationship in mission, and may thus lead to a tendency in social action programs to neglect the communication of the gospel. Even if this should be the case, the theology of Christian integral mission with the two-pronged emphasis on evangelism and social responsibility may still be conceptually right. It may therefore be justified to develop more specific mechanisms that might be introduced to ensure that a balance between evangelism and social action is maintained and that both proclamation and social service aspects become integral parts of Christian social action operations. It might be useful if, for example, some guidelines could be offered to create an awareness in church missions and specialized NGOs as to the place of gospel communication within the framework of social action programs of whatever nature, and on how various types of programs may be effectively linked up with local churches.

---

80. David Lowes Watson, "The Church As Journalist: Evangelism in the Context of the Local Church in the United States," *International Review of Mission* 72 (1983), 68.

2.4 Some Effects of the Lausanne Process

The major result of the Lausanne conference in 1974 may have been that "it dealt a deathblow to every attempt to reduce the mission of the church to the multiplication of Christians and churches through evangelism."[81] One immediate result of Lausanne was that there was an increased involvement by evangelicals in relief and development agencies around the world. As people in evangelical movements started to explore the implications of the new aspects of evangelical missiology that had been introduced at the Lausanne conference there was a mixed reception: some received an immediate backing from their own churches whereas others were met with a lack of interest and a cold shoulder.[82]

The integrated mission concept is today applied in relation to many different forms of Christian work. As the nature of the *microfinance* activities carried out by Christian organizations also takes many different forms, and all claim to be "Christian mission," it seems necessary to try to give specific content regarding what "mission" is on the operational level of mission activity.

2.4.1 A Paradigm Shift in the Theology of Mission

Integral mission thinking evolved initially as individuals within the evangelical tradition wanted to integrate the proclamation of the gospel and inviting people to accept Christ as Lord and Saviour with subsequent social action leading to transformation of social structures and justice.[83]

One important achievement of the Lausanne movement is that there is still today, forty years after the Lausanne conference, a broad consensus in the evangelical church regarding the integral mission concept as a basis for Christian mission. However, no Christian movement can survive on the achievements of the past. It requires a great deal of discipline in the behaviour of the church to ensure that the mandate to proclaim the gospel verbally will continue to be honoured in the new generation of Christians who have inherited the integral mission concept and who have enthusiastically become

---

81. C. René Padilla, in C. René Padilla and Chris Sugden, eds, *How Evangelicals Endorsed Social Responsibility* (Bramcote: Grove, 1985). Texts Vol. 2, 11.

82. Christopher Sugden, "Evangelicals and Wholistic Evangelism," in Vinay Samuel and Albrecht Hauser, *Proclaiming Christ in Christ's Way: Studies in Integral Mission* (Eugene: Wipf & Stock, 1989), 30.

83. E.g. Samuel and Hauser, *Proclaiming Christ*, 10.

involved in social action programs in the church at large. A failure to do so may result in an increased lack of coherence in evangelical mission thinking.

It is argued by Vinay Samuel and Albrecht Hauser that all the new models of integral evangelism were committed to keeping evangelism and social concern together and thus respond to the needs of the whole person. There was a sharp focus on the poor and justice.[84] The new movement had not only spokespeople from the Western world, but also a large number from the two-thirds world, with their first-hand experience of social injustice, poverty and deprivation. They were aware that as Christians they had to come up with satisfactory answers to the needs of the whole of humanity if they were to be listened to and become a vital and vibrant voice in their own societies. This demanded more theological reflection than maintaining a gospel of individualism and the need to find a synthesis of the two key commandments given by Christ: "Love your neighbour as yourself" and "go and make disciples" (Matt 22:39; 28:19).[85] Thus it was not only evangelicals in the Anglo-Saxon tradition who were a part of this movement. In Germany Walter Arnold maintained that the *raison d'être* for the existence of the church is holistic mission which includes evangelism.[86]

The Grand Rapids Consultation has been perceived by some as the approximate time when the tide in mission thinking had moved conclusively in favour of a paradigm shift in the evangelical church's concept of mission. Integral mission thinking has since pervaded Christian mission work all over the globe. It has had a number of effects, among them a steep increase in Christian NGOs and Christian faith-based voluntary societies of all kinds dedicated to kingdom work all over the world.[87] One demonstration of this was the rise of the Micah Network, a broad-based cooperation between churches, mission societies and Christian social action groups based on a common understanding of the integral mission concept as defined in the Micah Declaration. The Micah Network serves as an example of the impact of the integral mission concept.

---

84. Ibid., 12.

85. John Stott, cited in Dudley-Smith, *John Stott*, 211.

86. Walter Arnold, Interview on 22 February 1989, cited by Albrecht Hauser in Vinay and Albrecht, *Proclaiming Christ*, 25.

87. C. René Padilla, in *Dictionary of Mission Theology*, ed. John Corrie (Downers Grove: IVP, 2007), 158.

2.4.2 The Micah Declaration and Micah Network

The Lausanne Declaration was brought into the life of missions and NGOs in many different ways. One important such step was the establishment of the Micah Network in 1999 based on the mandate given in Micah 6:8: "What does the LORD require of you but to do justice, and to love kindness, and to walk humbly with your God?"[88] The organization, with its more than 330 member organizations and around 230 associate members, has a clear focus on integral mission with an emphasis on social services clearly expressed in their "vision statement" and the "Aims and Methods of the organization."[89] The Micah Network is based on the Micah Declaration on integral mission which in turn is derived from the integral mission thinking developed through the Lausanne process. In the years just prior to the setting up of the Micah Network the Anglican church had launched a holistic definition of mission called "Five Marks of Mission,"[90] which may have been influential in the shaping of the Micah Declaration.

Although the Micah Declaration initially states that integral mission is viewed as *the proclamation and demonstration of the gospel* the rest of the declaration concerns the identification of Jesus Christ with the oppressed. The opening three words of the statement do imply that evangelism and social involvement are separate activities,[91] but thereafter the text is a call to social involvement in a miserable world by walking with the poor, concern about globalization and the need to strengthen the lifestyle of Christians. The Micah Declaration, however, seems to take for granted that the proclamation of the gospel will be achieved as an integral part of social action programs.

There is an apparent lack of guidance in the declaration as to the need to keep evangelism and social responsibility together, mutually reinforcing one another. It may be asked if it is this somewhat superficial treatment of the proclamation part of integral mission in important statements such as the Micah Declaration that might make officers in various missions and Christian NGO missions more liable to drift into a lack of differentiation

---

88. The background to the creation of the Micah Network was a felt need in the evangelical community to integrate Christian social action programs in their mission activities by applying the integral mission concept of the Lausanne movement.

89. Micah Network, http://www.micahnetwork.org.

90. Anglican Communion, http://www.anglicancommunion.org/ministry/mission/fivemarks.cfm; accessed 11 November 2010.

91. Micah Network, http://www.micahnetwork.org/; accessed 4 March 2010.

between social service and evangelism, equating the two and easily ending up with social service only.

2.5 The Need for a Final Clarification of the Integral Mission Concept

The long process of accommodation of the integral mission concept since the Lausanne conference in 1974 has ensured that there is a broad consensus in the evangelical church with respect to the importance of employing the integral mission concept as a basis for Christian mission work. Although there is a broad consensus that mission involves proclamation of the gospel and social action to embody it, there is, however, still a lack of clarity and some discussion among evangelical theologians as to the priority of evangelism.

As the church is left with a more open-ended mission mandate it is quite possible that the introduction of the integral mission concept, in the absence of mechanisms to ensure a clear maintenance of proclamation in ongoing mission operations, has provided the church with a less clear-cut operational concept for mission.

This effect may have been reinforced by the influence of prevailing cultural factors on both integral mission activities and on the Christian personnel involved in the operations, in particular when a local culture is not only unreceptive but also rather hostile to Christianity. On the other hand, as the preceding discussion has shown, the case for doing Christian social action programs without evangelism has scant support in the covenants and statements of evangelical conferences in the context of the Lausanne process. It is also significant that some serious attempts have been made in the context of the Lausanne process to rectify the situation. These efforts have in particular been related to a clarification of the exact relationship between evangelism and social action over a timescale in the context of the local community so as to make the integral mission concept more operational in integral mission activities.

An important step toward a final clarification might be the "ultimacy" of evangelism concept if the concept is *expanded* and integrated in a committed and planned effort along a timescale in a local community context. Additionally, if the "ultimacy" of evangelism is expanded in this way it may be argued that this concept is quite akin to the "priority" of evangelism concept if "priority" is defined as something that should never be left undone.

Given the problems that the two concepts of "primacy" and "ultimacy" of evangelism raise it may, however, be useful to continue the search for a better word. With respect to "ultimacy" it is primarily the lack of a time dimension which makes it unsatisfactory from an operational point of view. An alternative might be the term "anticipation" of evangelism which can have a number of relevant meanings. The "act of anticipating" or "the state of being anticipated" reflects a realization in advance. In the area of law it can signify "a premature withdrawal or assignment of money from a trust estate." In music it could be "a tone introduced in advance of its harmony so that it sounds against the preceding chord."[92] Furthermore, "anticipation" has an element of emotion, possibly even of enthusiasm, as it is in anticipation that we consider a longed-for good event. Eschatologically, Christian mission is about Christians bringing the message of Christ concerning the anticipated arrival of the kingdom of God to others with an anticipation that it will be received and believed. It may be maintained that this anticipation should also characterize Christian social action in an integral mission context.

The use of "anticipation" might thus reflect the view that social action may create a bridge for evangelism, and also take care of the concern of many that evangelism should ultimately not be left out. "Anticipation" contains a stronger reference to a time and planning element than the "ultimacy" concept as it implies a more known and thus more specific time horizon from the initiation of a social action to the introduction of an evangelism element, as evangelism is anticipated. The opposite is non-anticipation, which is more what "ultimacy" may reflect as it is without a time horizon. Hence social action in integral mission in a local community would be anticipative of evangelism.

The principle of "anticipation" may be applied in a variety of Christian social action settings which are often complex with respect to the communication of the gospel. Anders Bergem argues that a Christian helper is committed in relation to three different value systems.[93] In his view the first commitment is to work in concurrence with the values of that particular area of work and profession; the second is to have a profound respect for the client; while the third is the commitment in relation to God, a relationship that includes a view of reality resulting from the knowledge of the revelation of God to humanity. With respect to Christian testimony in the context of a work operation the issue to be discussed is the relationship between the first two and the last commitment. He maintains that in Christianity the

---

92. "Anticipation," Dictionary.com, http://dictionary.reference.com/browse/anticipation; accessed 14 May 2010.

93. Anders Bergem, *Kristen Tro og profesjonell omsorg* (trans. from Norwegian: Christian Faith and Professional Care; Oslo: Luther forlag, 1998), 184.

communication of the divine has a value that exceeds everything else, as it relates directly to human life both in this world and beyond earthly life. Notwithstanding this, however, Bergem concludes that the reality of the incarnation implies that a Christian is obligated not to use a position of power in a client relationship to exercise pressure through a professional link to a person. The reason is that even the best intention (e.g. 1 Tim 2:3–4) cannot justify the exercise of pressure from a Christian helper that carries with it a negation of the freedom of another person to be solely responsible for his or her own life and relationship to God.[94]

In this perspective a Christian worker would exercise qualitative judgement with respect to the integral mission objective to communicate the gospel. This would be true whether the client is a patient or a client in a microfinance organization. Whether a Christian testimony in word is communicated or not, the integral mission concept based on anticipation would imply that the Christian helper would always hope and anticipate that at some point the knowledge of the incarnation will be communicated to the client, while at the same time being committed to being as instrumental as possible in that process based on the principles discussed above.

2.6 Conclusion

Notwithstanding the discussions on the priority of evangelism, the Lausanne Covenant and the subsequent deliberations on the relationship between social action and evangelism in integral mission have confirmed that the evangelical church maintains that its mandate is unchanged to proclaim the gospel of Christ in word and to embody it in social action with a view to improving the life situation of the poor and oppressed. Without an element of verbal proclamation of the gospel in the context of social action the latter may have beneficial social effects, but is not Christian mission as defined in the course of the Lausanne process.

I therefore argue that it is justified to judge the operations of churches and Christian NGOs in social action both on whether the operations meet the needs of the poor and protect their material and social interests, and on whether *it may be anticipated that the gospel of Christ will be proclaimed*, meeting the deepest spiritual human needs. The following chapters will be an assessment of the extent to which contemporary Christian microfinance

---

94. Ibid., 193.

operations satisfy these requirements and of how shortcomings may be rectified in relation to the integral mission concept.

3

Microfinance in Christian Mission and Perceived Effects on the Poor

The objective of this chapter is to establish a basis for an empirical study to appraise the potential of Christian microfinance as a vehicle in Christian integral mission. The goal is to identify the main drivers for mission drift in Christian microfinance in relation to the biblical perspectives for the poor and poverty in an integral mission framework as defined through the Lausanne process. I also raise the question whether Christian microfinance is directed at the poor and has the potential to alleviate their situation in relation to both material and spiritual poverty.

The chapter gives an account of the role and performance of microfinance in social action as a means to enable people to break out of material poverty. It also questions whether microfinance may constitute a platform for spiritual transformation strategies. We then go on to consider in more detail the key drivers of mission drift in relation to helping the poorest in material terms as well as in relation to spiritual transformation.

3.1 Microfinance

There has been a major shift in the market for microfinance in that from being primarily a philanthropic movement dominated by NGOs, it has now become a major industry such that multinational banks such as Citibank see microfinance as a profit opportunity. Several microfinance institutions have been transformed from charities to profitable companies through initial offerings (IPOs), the best known being the notorious Compartamos in Mexico, whose owners used a USD 6 million investment to become a billion dollar company within a few years by charging very high interest rates. "Thus what was once an idealistic movement is now a fast-growing industry, and one that is rapidly losing its innocence."[1] It is within this market framework that Christian microfinance institutions will operate in the future, and it is thus in relation to this industry that Christian microfinance will endeavour to make a difference by embracing and communicating values as vehicles of integral mission.

The microfinance market is heterogeneous and includes a large number of different institutional categories so that a regulated Microfinance Organization (MFO) could take the form of a stockholding company, bank, finance company, NGO, credit union, and so on. The heterogeneity of the organizations operating in the market makes it hard to assess the size of it, and estimates vary considerably. The Microfinance Information Exchange (MIX) indicated that worldwide, as per 31 December 2009, there were 1,395 MFOs which were MIX-registered and which in total were extending loans estimated at USD 44.2 billion to 86.2 million credit clients. The growth in the microfinance market is considerable: the gross loan portfolio of the MFOs increased at a compound average rate of 34.2 percent in the period 2003–2008.[2]

Microfinance is considered by many – such as the United Nations Millennium Project, an independent advisory body commissioned by the UN General Secretary – to be one of the most important vehicles available to governments in order to reach the first six out of the seven Millennium Goals, particularly Millennium Goal 1: Reduce the proportion of people living in extreme poverty by half between 1990 and 2015.[3]

3.2 A Biblical Context for "the Poor" in Microfinance

Although this is not the place to go deeply into the extensive literature on poverty or causes of poverty, some considerations of the complexity in defining the nature of poverty are necessary as the poor are the key target

---

1. Tim Harford, "The Battle for the Soul of Microfinance," *FT Magazine*, 6 December 2008, http://www.ft.com/cms/s/0/8080c698-c0d2-11dd-b0a8-000077b07658.html.

2. Adrian Gonzalez, "Microfinance at a Glance – 2008. Updated on December 31, 2009," Microfinance Information Exchange (MIX), http://www.themix.org/sites/default/files/Microfinance%20at%20a%20Glance%202009-12-31.pdf; accessed 4 May 2010.

3. "We Can End Poverty: Millennium Development Goals and Beyond 2015," United Nations, http://www.un.org/millenniumgoals/; accessed 6 November 2010.

group of Christian microfinance: its *raison d'être* is to improve the material and spiritual situation of the poor. Hence, in order to establish whether mission drift occurs in relation to this main objective of microfinance, it is useful to establish some notion or quantitative expression of who the poor are. The complexities of understanding the mechanisms producing poverty also throw light on what microfinance can and cannot do when it comes to improving the situation of the poor.

Also, the biblical perspectives on the poor are relevant when assessing Christian initiatives in this area. The contention of the practitioners of Christian microfinance is that microfinance may enable poor people to break out of the poverty cycle. One of the main charges against Christian microfinance, and against microfinance in general, is that the client base increasingly tends to be better off than originally planned, and well above the absolute poverty line.[4]

Microfinance is a matter both of helping the poor and of carrying out the operations to help the poor in a way that does not negatively impact the vulnerable party in the transactions. Hence the purpose of the following paragraphs is to identify a concept of "the poor" that is related in a practical way to what microfinance seeks to achieve, and not to explore the many facets of "poverty" and "the poor." Neither is this the place to make an attempt at reviewing the social and economic mechanisms that produce poverty, nor to discuss the many views on how poverty may be eradicated.

For the purpose of this study it suffices to say that the contemporary concept of poverty – who "the poor" are – is often relative. For the OECD the term "poverty line" describes an income level "considered minimally sufficient to sustain a family in terms of food, housing, clothing, medical needs, and so on,"[5] and relative poverty occurs "when total household income is less than half of the national net income average of the working population."[6] The World Bank employs the term "absolute poverty" for an income of below USD 1.25 a day (in 2005 prices), which is considered a minimum requirement for physical survival. This poverty threshold corresponds to the average poverty

---

4. Jesila M. Ledesma and Ma. Chona O. David-Casis, *Mission First: SPM Advocacy in the Philippines* (Pasig City: Microfinance Council of the Philippines, 2010), 6.

5. "Poverty Line: Glossary of Statistical Terms," OECD, http://stats.oecd.org/glossary/detail. asp?ID=6337; accessed May 4, 2010.

6. "When Money Is Tight: Poverty Dynamics in OECD Countries," OECD Employment Outlook, OECD, http://www.oecd.org/dataoecd/29/55/2079296.pdf, p. 41; accessed 4 May, 2010.

line found in the fifteen poorest countries in the world in terms of per capita consumption. "Poverty" is defined as an income of less than USD 2 per day, corresponding to the median poverty line for a larger group of developing countries (based on 2005 Purchasing Power Parity terms).[7] These measures are used to compare poverty across countries and over time, and to assess progress in poverty alleviation.

In the NT several different Greek words are used to describe the poor, being needy and poverty: *ptochos*, *penes*, *endees* and *penichros*.[8] Although there may be a semantic overlap between these words their use in the NT still indicates some differences of meaning. *Ptochos* is the word used for "being poor and destitute, implying a continuous state" (Jas 2:2), whereas *penes* is used in 2 Corinthians 9:9: "he scatters abroad, he gives to the poor, his righteousness endures for ever," quoting Psalm 112:9 and describing a poor person, probably someone less poor than one who is *ptochos*. The person who is *endees* – as used in Acts 4:34, "there was not a needy person among them" – is in a similar state to one who is *ptochos*, but due to a serious lack of resources required for living rather than a continuous state of destitution. The use of *penichros* describes a person who lacks the essential means of livelihood, as reflected in Luke 21:2: "and he saw a poor widow putting in two copper coins."

The position of the poor as a key target group for Christian mission is further enhanced by Christ when, as narrated by Luke, he referred to Isaiah 61:1–2 in the synagogue of Nazareth: "The Spirit of the Lord is upon me, because he has anointed me to preach good news to the poor . . . to proclaim the acceptable year of the Lord" (Luke 4:16–19). Joel B. Green argues that although there is no historical evidence to suggest that the jubilee was ever executed, it had not been forgotten by Israel, and Luke introduces Christ's opening address as "an announcement of the final jubilee, the era of salvation, the breaking point of God's kingdom."[9] The gospel proclaimed by Christ may thus have been linked to the OT teaching of the jubilee that was introduced to give people mired in debt a chance to start anew with their lives, thereby extending to them an opportunity to escape from the poverty trap. The Greek

---

7. World Bank Institute, "Basic Poverty Measurement and Analysis Course: Poverty Lines (Module 3)," http://info.worldbank.org/etools/docs/library/207203/Module3.pdf; accessed 5 November 2010.

8. Eugene A. Nida and Johannes P. Louw, *Greek–English Lexicon of the New Testament Based on Semantic Domains*, Vol. 1 (New York: United Bible Societies, 1988–89), 564. Sections 57.49–51 and 57.53.

9. Joel B. Green, *The Theology of the Gospel of Luke* (New Testament Theology; Cambridge: Cambridge University Press, 1995), 78.

word used in Luke 4:16 translated as "poor" is *ptochos*, describing people in a permanent state of poverty. In order to reflect an important target group for Christian mission as described by Christ, Christian microfinance would do well to keep a focus on those groups in the population that are far down on the poverty ladder in society. However, in the context of the NT, "the poor" are not to be understood as a socio-economic group only in terms of contemporary measures for material poverty as Jesus also frequently applies the word "poor" to people who have a dishonourable status in society, the excluded.[10] At times, economically deprived people far down the material poverty ladder in a society tend to overlap with the groups that suffer from exclusion or low social status.

In the NT compassion is thus expressed both toward people who are described in Greek as *ptochos* and toward those who are described as *penes*, although the latter group seemed to have a living standard somewhat higher than those living in a permanent state of absolute poverty, *ptochos*. It may therefore be argued that a target group defined as "poor" might be those on an income sustaining a household per capita income consumption up about USD 2 per day, that is, somewhat exceeding the level of income which indicates a state of absolute poverty. It should be kept in mind that pre-industrial Palestine at the time of Christ was a poor agricultural country in twenty-first century terms and most people were poor in terms of twenty-first century categories. Yet the focus of Christ was on those who lacked basic amenities in the most crucial areas of life, food and shelter. Today, people who suffer that degree of deprivation would be located some way down on the poverty ladder in a society, although not necessarily at the bottom. Biblical inspiration and a basis for the effort to focus on helping "the poor" to break out of the poverty cycle may also be drawn from other texts in the NT. Some of them clarify the obligation of the church and individual Christians to help mitigate the dire situation of the poor. In Luke 16:19–31 we read the story of the rich man who did not take notice of the sufferings of the beggar Lazarus. The core message of the story seems to be that the followers of Christ are obligated to respond in a positive manner to the visible plight of the poor. In Matthew 25:31–46 Christ uses a metaphor to describe the righteous as those who have fed the hungry, who gave the thirsty water to drink, who provided clothes when seeing a stranger naked or who expressed care for prisoners. This parable is widely used to underpin the need for social action to help the

---

10. Ibid., 82.

poor, but it is particularly difficult to understand the meaning because Christ did not give any interpretation of it.[11] Throughout church history there have been two main interpretations. One is that "the least of these my brethren" (Matt 25:40) refers to the disciples of Jesus; thus the parable teaches that those who should be cared for are Christians in need.[12] The second interpretation is that these words refer to "anyone in need." Craig L. Blomberg contends that the prevailing interpretation that Jesus teaches about the need to help people whether or not they are Christians is correct, thus questioning the view that limits the use of the metaphor to helping only Christian poor.[13]

Gray's comprehensive study of the history of interpretation of this parable shows that the great majority of commentators in the nineteenth and twentieth century who understood the parable to refer to the last judgement also stated that "the little ones" should be understood in the widest sense. For example, in the twentieth century, 305 authors out of 440 listed names maintained that "the least" referred to "everyone."[14] Gray also maintains that the tendency in the twentieth century toward a more universal interpretation of verse 40 is a result of the suffering that accompanied the two world wars, and of the second Vatican Council, which influenced the growth of the universalist interpretation. However, Gray himself believes that Christ refers to Christians in need, as elsewhere in Matthew, when Christ uses the word "brother," he designates members of the community of believers. Gray argues that there is no reason to believe that it has another meaning in this particular parable.

Whichever view – the restrictive or the universal interpretation – is correct, other parts of the NT (e.g. the parable of the good Samaritan, Luke 10:30–37, and the injunction to "love your neighbour as yourself," Mark 12:31) indicate that Christians should feel compassion for poor and needy people and should act compassionately whatever their ethnicity or background.

The above brief summary of the way the poor are described in the NT underlines the need to target households falling below the prevailing

---

11. George Eldon Ladd, "The Parable of the Sheep and the Goats in Recent Interpretation," in Richard N. Longernecker and Merrill C. Tenney, eds., *New Dimensions in New Testament Study* (Grand Rapids: Zondervan, 1974), 191.

12. Ibid., 197.

13. Craig L. Blomberg, *Neither Poverty Nor Riches: A Biblical Theology of Possessions* (Downers Grove: Inter-Varsity Press, 1999), 126.

14. Sherman W. Gray, *The Least of My Brothers: Matthew 25.31–46: A History of Interpretation* (Atlanta: Scholars Press, 1989), 257.

thresholds for poverty, but it also shows that there is no strict definition in the NT of who the poor are.

It is thus imperative for Christian microfinance to have a focus on the poor. Although a poor person may be as resourceful in personal terms as others, that person does not have access to the same financial and social resource base as other citizens. The poor also tend to lack social and political power and are therefore not easily able to change their situation through political processes. Hence, at the level of microfinance, "the poor" require a number of services (e.g. counselling and educational services) in addition to benefiting from the financial instruments of microfinance. Such advisory services aimed at enhancing the capacity of poor clients to service their loans become particularly important when it is kept in mind that debt has some dark sides to it; it may be the cause of social disruption and decay, and may also lead people deeper into debt and breed many other social ills.[15]

Given the focus on the poor in the NT there is therefore a need for every Christian MFO to define the poor as a target group as clearly as possible within the cultural context in which it operates. This is particularly important as there tends to be commercial pressure on the MFOs to focus on clients higher up the poverty ladder, partly because they tend to be easier to serve, but also because the risk of loan losses is lower and the loan amounts may be higher when lending to better-off poor clients, thus lowering the operational costs of the enterprise.

A softening of the stance to focus on "the poor" with a subsequent shift to focusing the mission on groups higher up the income ladder might therefore indicate a mission drift At this juncture it is important to point out that the clients will normally not be the abject poor – the handicapped, elderly people, those who are not able to work, also called the "ultra poor." The borrower must have the personal resource potential to repay a loan that has been used to implement a project.[16] Thus, even if microfinance should be a powerful poverty reduction mechanism, it is not a panacea for the removal of every pocket of poverty in a country.

---

15. Jamie A. Grant and Dewi A. Hughes, *Transforming the World? The Gospel and Social Responsibility* (Nottingham: Inter-Varsity Press, 2009), 85.

16. Andrew Kirk, *What Is Mission? Theological Explorations* (Minneapolis: Fortress Press, 2000), 97.

3.3 The Nature of Poverty

The discussion in the previous section shows that the task of defining in detail the target group itself, the "poor," is fraught with problems. The view we have of poverty and the nature of it will impact the way we try to help and assist the poor. Hence there is a need to define more precisely the nature of poverty. The following discussion looks at the social and spiritual aspects of poverty.

3.3.1 Socio-Economic Aspects of Poverty

The causes of poverty may be linked to the nature of poverty in a variety of ways – for example, to social structures, lack of access to the financial system, lack of assets, and lack of power and ability to change the situation. However, there is no consensus view on who the "poor" are and what causes poverty. One reason for this is that poverty is multifaceted. This is clear from the many attempts that have been made at capturing the essence of poverty in terms of theoretical models. For example, one leading development expert, Robert Chambers, prefers to describe poverty in terms of households that are powerless and not capable of breaking out of the "poverty trap."[17] This approach to the understanding of the nature and causes of poverty is useful in that it gives the family unit a key role in an interactive system of five interlocking parts, each of which describes an aspect of the situation of the poor: *material poverty*, reflecting the lack of an asset base; *physical weakness*, reflecting lack of health services and so on; *isolation*, indicating that individuals are excluded from the educational and financial system; *vulnerability*, reflecting a high degree of sensitivity to changing circumstances such as floods, and limited reserves and choices; and *powerlessness*, reflecting their lack of political influence in society and their exposure to exploitation. The essence of Chambers' thinking seems to be that the various parts reinforce each other and capture households in the grip of poverty.

The tendency to consider poverty in terms of households may also be found in other development thinkers. John Friedman offers an analytical apparatus that consists of four overlapping domains in society that embed the poor – the political community, the state, civil society and the corporate

---

17. Robert Chambers, *Rural Development: Putting the Last First* (London: Longman, 1983), 103.

economy – as he also views the household as the core unit of a civic society.[18] He carefully describes a number of social limitations which impact the absolute poor in society as they are not able to exercise sufficient influence to improve their situation, whether in relation to their social networks, financial resources, free time, instruments of work and livelihood, knowledge and skills and possibilities for self-development; in other words, the poor are basically characterized by powerlessness and lack of access to social power.[19]

Thus there seems to be the common understanding of poverty that it embraces a network of complicated interlocking areas of life, both at the individual level and at the level of society. To complicate the picture even further, poverty may also be understood in terms of inequalities in the global systems that regulate trade, investments and other financial flows that affect the poor in whichever country they are located.

3.3.2 Spiritual Aspects of Poverty

The theories and concepts described above illustrate that there is a poverty cycle which it is hard for an individual or a household to break out of. However, although the poor may be described in terms of their economic and social situation, it is also clear that they do not rely solely on material improvements in terms of more consumption and services for their happiness. Joel B. Green documents that when Jesus preaches "good news to the poor," this is not just a matter of helping people materially, but in a broader sense it is related to bringing "release."[20] He contends that the "release" effect is of great significance in understanding Jesus' ministry and that "Luke portrays both forgiveness and healing in social terms to match their more evident spiritual and physical overtones."[21] He goes on to say that the use of the word "blind" has a broader meaning than describing the literal physical condition; it is also a metaphor used in the context of receiving release and salvation and inclusion in the family of God.[22] Thus in a biblical context poverty is clearly multifaceted.

---

18. John Friedman, *Empowerment: The Politics of Alternative Development* (Cambridge: Blackwell, 1992), 26–29.

19. Ibid., 67.

20. Green, *Theology of the Gospel of Luke*, 78.

21. Ibid., 79.

22. Ibid.

It is argued by Bryant Myers that without a strong theology of sin it is hard to find a comprehensive explanation for poverty and that the cause of poverty is fundamentally spiritual.[23] A basic explanatory factor for the entrapment of the poor is sin in society which impedes the possibilities of the poor. As has been demonstrated by the studies referred to in section 3.3.1 above, strong stakeholders in a society employ their power to suppress the poor. Bryant Myers argues that sin has marred all relationships, and he describes the fundamental causes of poverty in the following way: "Poverty is the result of relationships that do not work, that are not just, that are not for life, that are not harmonious or enjoyable. Poverty is the absence of shalom in all its meanings."[24] He argues that the good news is that through Jesus Christ there is a way out of sin through transformation, but accepts that if this is not accepted the situation will be unchanged by self-imposed limitations.[25] He further maintains that this has an obvious implication for Christian social action work, as Christian transformational development work also means that people should in some form hear the good news of the gospel and be given the chance to respond.[26]

The spiritual aspects of poverty will be further discussed in section 3.6.2.

3.4 Targeting Material Poverty Reduction in Microfinance

None of the general analytical concepts briefly described above are of much help, however, when it comes to measuring mission drift in microfinance on the level of microfinance lending, as "mission drift" in the product delivery system of microfinance would best be assessed on a quantifiable basis. Although an increase or decrease in a quantifiable factor may not explain changes in overall poverty due to its complex structure, a quantifiable factor may still be a viable measure in so far as it can indicate, although in an imprecise way, which way microfinance is going in terms of relating to the poor as a target group.

Thus, if poverty were defined in terms of "powerlessness," it would be necessary to measure the result of intervention from microfinance on the basis of the impact on social relations and the underlying causes of power

---

23. Bryant L. Myers, *Walking with the Poor: Principles and Practices of Transformational Development* (New York: Orbis, 2008), 88.

24. Ibid., 86.

25. Ibid., 88.

26. Ibid.

relations that are detrimental to the poor. However, "powerlessness" and similar notions have unclear definitions and hence are difficult to measure. It is therefore difficult to determine the effect of MFO interventions in relation to economic and social inequalities that are structural in nature, but without such evidence on the effects of microfinance outreach it is hard to establish a record for microfinance activities on poverty reduction.[27]

3.4.1 Measurement of Effects of Microfinance on Income and Vulnerability

Thus a good poverty indicator would have to be objective, verifiable and easy to collect. Concern for mission drift is widespread in the industry and there has therefore been a search for proxy indicators[28] which may be used to assess depth of outreach.[29] Outreach is measured by the width of the geographical impact of financial products whereas indepth targeting measures the extent to which a program reaches the poorest.

It is widely accepted that evaluation of the effect of social action mechanisms such as microfinance on the whole web of interacting poverty-generating relationships, whether political, cultural or economic in nature, is methodologically complex. There is therefore a need to use simpler measurements which may give indications of the impact of microfinance interventions on poverty. This may be defended simply on the grounds that several of the poverty-generating mechanisms, such as lack of assets, lack of reserves to protect against vulnerability (Robert Chambers) or lack of access to economic power (John Friedman), may be favourably impacted if microfinance interventions lead to an improved asset and income base and/ or reduce vulnerability.

One such approach is to conceive of poverty as a low level of annual income per person. Poverty reduction would then be measured "by counting the number or proportion of people who cross that line – who are promoted out of poverty."[30] Poverty estimates released in August 2008 showed that about 1.4 billion people in the developing world were living on less than

---

27. James Copestake, Martin Greely, Susan Johnson, Naila Kabeer and Anton Simanowitz, *Money with a Mission: Microfinance and Poverty Reduction* (Bourton-on-Dunsmore: ITDG, 2005), 25.

28. A proxy indicator is an indirect measure that approximates a phenomenon in the absence of a direct measure.

29. Copestake et al., *Money with a Mission*, 27.

30. Susan Johnson and Ben Rogaly, *Microfinance and Poverty Reduction* (Oxford: Oxfam and Action Aid, 1997), 10.

USD 1.25 per day.[31] In practical terms this means lack of shelter, hunger, poor health services, unemployment, powerlessness, and so on. However, the USD 1.25 or USD 2 per day is a deceptive threshold for an MFO in operational terms. It is difficult to pre-target the poor living on less than USD 1.25 or USD 2 a day as the exact income level of poor households in poor countries cannot be read from public statistics and is generally not available. Hence it might be advantageous for both the MFO and the borrowers to target whole communities when the communities themselves in general would tend to have households living below the poverty line.

Also, if poverty is understood in terms of vulnerability it would be possible to employ a quantitative measure. When viewing poverty in terms of vulnerability one important objective of microfinance would be to carry the borrowers through temporary fluctuations in income, also called "consumption smoothing."[32] Such downturns may be expected, caused by seasonal variations of crops, or unexpected, caused by floods, crop failures, and so on. Poverty reduction will be achieved to the extent that the degree of vulnerability of households to such expected or unexpected fluctuations in income is reduced.

It follows from this that different views of poverty have implications for microfinance programs. If a program is conceived as being successful if it raises average income, the program will be designed with this objective in view. If the prime objective of the microfinance program is to reduce vulnerability, then improving the capacity of the household clients of the program to come through expected or unexpected fluctuations in income will determine the lending policies and define the degree of success. The importance of differences in the objectives of microfinance programs has been demonstrated by a study carried out by Hulme and Mosley which indicated that the better the asset and skill base of the borrowers, the greater the increase in income from a microfinance loan.[33] This would suggest that those who already have assets and skills are able to make better use of the loans. The study also showed that the poorest are less able to increase their

---

31. The World Bank, http://web.worldbank.org/WBSITE/EXTPOVERTY/0.print:Y; accessed 26 March 2010.

32. "Consumption smoothing" is often used in microfinance literature to describe loans that alleviate acute financial crises for the poor which, in the absence of microfinance loans, might force a family into the embrace of a moneylender. E.g. David Ellerman, in Dichter and Harper, *What's Wrong with Microfinance?*, 153.

33. D. Hulme and P. Mosley, *Finance Against Poverty*, 2 vols. (London: Routledge, 1996), 2; cited in Johnson and Rogaly, *Microfinance and Poverty Reduction*, 11–12.

incomes. Furthermore, the study indicated that some of the poorest clients ended up worse off than before they obtained the loan as they were not able to repay it. This exposed them to high risks in a vulnerable situation. Hulme and Mosley's study indicated that the extension of credit to micro-enterprises is unlikely to help the poor to raise their incomes. However, easy access to credit may help poor people to cope with income fluctuations. Reduction of vulnerability is, however, not necessarily a way of breaking out of the poverty cycle, although it may be contended that it makes life in poverty more bearable. Against this background it seems appropriate to consider carefully what the poorest clients really need.

The importance of structuring and designing products that protect the poor clients and further their interests had been underlined by reports of suicides following the seizure of assets of poor people who were not able to repay.[34] These were people who had taken up credits which they were unable to service according to contract. The MFOs should ensure that the credit product offered to a client can be repaid by an expected income stream, thus protecting the client against the effects of a default, which may be tragic. The many suicides committed by microfinance clients in India suggest that some MFOs in that country did not take sufficiently seriously their social responsibility as credit institutions for poor people.

One reason for applying quantitative measures of poverty reduction is that limited access to the financial system is one of many factors which keep the poor within the poverty trap. Thus to the extent that microfinance may help to empower poor households financially, and thereby also improve their access to other important areas in society, it will have an explicit effect on the situation of the poor.

3.5 Microfinance: Does It Help the Poor?

When microcredit was launched it was widely held that it could eradicate poverty by giving poor people access to capital from which they had hitherto been excluded. With this perspective in mind many Christian NGOs, agencies and missions adopted microcredit as a form of social action.

---

34. Dr Sudhirendar Sharma, "Are Microfinance Institutions Exploiting the Poor?," Infochange: Poverty, August 2006, http://infochangeindia.org/20060802286/Poverty/ Analysis/Are-micro-finance-institutions-exploiting-the-poor.html; accessed 10 April 2010. The article reported that microfinance had taken its first toll of sixty lives in Andhra Pradesh in April 2006.

Over the years there have been many appraisals, evaluations of microfinance programs and overall assessments with a view to establishing their effects on the poor. Some of the major and most recent evaluations are reviewed below. There have also been some studies on mission drift in microfinance – that is, whether MFOs gradually target client groups that are better off than the very poor groups of the population originally targeted.[35]

Measuring the impact of microfinance is complicated as it needs to assess the counterfactual – to establish what would have happened to a person who borrowed money from an MFO if he or she had not done so. As will be shown in what follows, most studies endeavour to establish a control group who are non-borrowers. However, if borrowers at the outset are more entrepreneurial than non-borrowers, this will tend to overstate the effect of microfinance. In the following section is a summary of some of the main studies of possible mission drift in microfinance in general, and in Christian microfinance in particular, in relation to product delivery as well as in relation to overall Christian integrated mission objectives.

3.5.1 Result of Impact Studies in Microfinance

Although this is not the place to carefully appraise the significance of the many studies that have been made on microfinance, much of what is available tends to support the view that microfinance reduces the vulnerability of the poor. On the other hand, the studies have not, as many had advocated and hoped for, provided a basis for concluding that microfinance leads to a massive and large-scale reduction in poverty for the very poor. There are several reasons why impact studies indicate that the effect of microfinance on the income development of the poorest households has been rather limited.

First, a large number of the very poor are often destitute people who would be unlikely to be able to service a loan for whatever purpose it was intended. There is evidence that these poorest segments of the population are excluded from microfinance lending, including MFOs that have effective poverty-targeting instruments.[36] One important reason for such exclusion is the credit risk that an MFO would take if it should generally accept very

---

35. E.g. Mersland and Strøm, "Microfinance Mission Drift?"
36. S. V. Rangacharyulu, *Targeting of and Dropouts among SML Clients: A Report for the Centre for Quantitative Techniques* (Hyderabad: National Institute of Rural Development, 2004); cited by Martin Greeley, "Sustainable Poverty Outreach," in Copestake et al., *Money with a Mission*, 23.

poor groups as clients. Second, the poor clients tend to exclude themselves from borrowing as they do not consider themselves able to pay back a loan. These households simply do not have a cash flow that gives them a sufficient debt-service capacity. Third, if the MFO is operating a system with individual loans with a group collateral, the group tends to exclude the poorest clients as the group would have to pay up for clients who defaulted on their loans.

Some studies illustrate this picture. A major cross-sectional survey of nearly 1,800 households in Bangladesh was based on household-level data provided by the Bangladesh Institute of Development Studies. The study applied appropriate treatment/control frameworks to answer the question of effects on poverty.[37] Some households had access to microfinance whereas the control group was located in areas with no microfinance. The study showed that the most important potential impacts are associated with reduction in vulnerability, not with poverty reduction. A reduction in vulnerability has the effect of mitigating the exposure of poor households to external shocks that, for example, would lead to a sudden fall in their income. Poverty reduction is related to income growth which results in a higher material living standard. It is particularly interesting that when the normal simple estimates of the impact of microfinance without control groups were made, these showed clear achievement, indicating that they are driven entirely by selection bias. This means that the impact on incomes would have happened even in the absence of microfinance. At the time of the study this result contradicted the many frequent claims made about income effects of microfinance as it highlighted that there are real methodological difficulties connected with measuring the effects on income from microfinance credits.[38]

Another study was undertaken in Hyderabad, India, by a group of researchers from Massachusetts Institute of Technology (MIT) to determine the effect of access to microcredit.[39] The research was devised in such a way that participation in the program was determined primarily by chance. Fifty-two randomly chosen slums were given access to microfinance and fifty-two equally suitable other randomly chosen slums were denied such access. The researchers were thereby able to see the effect of microfinance on the whole

---

37. Jonathan Murdoch, "Does Microfinance Really Help the Poor? New Evidence from Flagship Programs in Bangladesh," published paper, Harvard University, 1998.

38. Ibid., 2.

39. Abhijit Banerjee, Esther Duflo, Rachel Glennerster and Cynthia Kinnan, "Measuring the Impact of Microfinance in Hyderabad, India," The Abdul Latif Jameel Poverty Action Lab, http://www.povertyactionlab.org/; accessed 11 November 2010.

community. The same approach was chosen by a group of researchers from Yale University in the Philippines.[40] Here also people with only marginal credit stories were chosen as clients. Neither study found that microfinance reduced poverty. Only one in five loans in the Hyderabad study led to the creation of a new business, and the researchers indicated that providing poor people with high-quality savings products might have a more beneficial effect in the long run.[41]

The issue of methodology is particularly difficult to solve when conducting studies of income effects from microfinance loans in local markets where there are several MFOs that compete and have some degree of client overlap in the market. In such market situations it is difficult to identify a control group which may be used in the assessment of the impact of microfinance on income levels and the livelihood of the borrowers.

The basic idea behind the microfinance movement has been that an important reason for poverty is that the poor have been excluded from credit, and that the inclusion of the poor in the credit system will therefore enable them to break out of the poverty cycle as they use borrowed funds to start micro-enterprises. Notwithstanding the positive experiences of many projects, the general experience of microfinance so far has tended to demonstrate that the majority of micro-borrowers use the proceeds from their loans for non-business purposes.[42] Not many are entrepreneurs, and many of the funds borrowed are used for consumption smoothing – that is, loans are used to carry the borrower through a period of hardship, to pay bills for the education of children, for painting the house, or for buying fertilizer or a plot of land. Much borrowing also replaces the private moneylenders and eases the financial pressures on borrowers of such funds.

40. Xavier Giné, Tomoko Harigaya, Dean Karlan et al, "Evaluating Microfinance Program Innovation with Randomized Control Trials: An Example from Group Versus Individual Lending," Yale University, March 2006, http://karlan.yale.edu/p/ADB_TN16.pdf; accessed 12 November 2010.

41. "Economic Focus: A Partial Marvel," The Economist, 16 July 2009, http://www.economist.com/node/14031284.

42. Richard Rosenberg, "Does Microcredit Really Help Poor People?", CGAP, 5 October 2009, http://www.cgap.org/blog/does-microcredit-really-help-poor-people; accessed 15 March 2010.

3.5.2 Comments on the Performance of Microfinance in Poverty Eradication

There needs to be a willingness in the microfinance industry to listen to its critics as the above data should not be unexpected. Dichter contends that in order to better understand some of the limitations of microfinance as a vehicle for economic growth and poverty reduction, it may be useful to draw on some lessons from the economic history of industrialized countries. The development of microfinance so far seems to be confirmed by the history of the now-rich countries in the world in which earlier forms of microcredit never had a major role when it came to business development. The economic development came before the movements to democratize credit, such as in the form of savings unions or savings banks. Also, when credit was extended to the poor it tended to follow the savings movements and was largely used in relation to consumption. Dichter concludes that the average person in the past and today is not on the whole an entrepreneur and credit is mostly used for consumption smoothing.[43]

Research also indicates that historically, formal bank credit was used by established businesses and that "access to formal credit by the poor follows savings and is for consumption, and that economic development and its consequent massive poverty reduction did not depend on microcredit being made more accessible."[44] Historically therefore, in the global North people tended to use the banks for their savings. Only at a later stage did the banks offer credits, and then it was primarily for consumption and not for investments. The credits offered were aimed for the low- and middle-income families to reduce the power of the loan shark. The experience of microfinance so far is not so unlike that which the history of the global North can teach us: only a few are entrepreneurs, and most of the microfinance borrowers just want to pay back their loans. These lessons may have important implications for the MFOs as it may not necessarily be beneficial always to reach very poor clients who are not likely to have the regular cash flow that enables them to make payments on the loan according to contract.

It should, however, be kept in mind that Dichter's main focus is primarily the macro-economic impacts of microfinance. Much of his criticism is based on knowledge of the pattern which the industrial countries followed in their

43. Thomas Dichter, "A Second Look at Microfinance: The Sequence of Growth and Credit in Economic History," Cato Institute, Washington DC Development Policy Briefing Paper, 15 February 2007, no.1, 1–2.
44. Ibid., 8.

economic development. However, there is no evidence that the development of the global South will follow the same pattern. It should also be kept in mind that the focus in Christian microfinance is on the effects on individuals in a community context, and general features that may hold true for the industry as a whole may not hold true for a given MFO. There seems to be enough evidence to maintain that microfinance does make it possible for large numbers of individuals to break out of poverty, although the most significant effect of microfinance seems to be the reduction of vulnerability.

Notwithstanding this general picture, MFOs from all around the world can document convincingly that many funds have been used for the promotion of entrepreneurs. Hence, although the general picture seems to be that consumption smoothing represents the lion's share of the capital disbursed, the number of people who have been able to set up self-sustaining businesses from loans is not insignificant. Unfortunately there is no data pool that can be accessed in order to get an exact description of the final usage of microfinance loans.

It may thus be concluded that studies that have been made of the effects of microfinance on poverty indicate, first, that the poverty reduction impact is less than expected, and second, that most microfinance is for consumption smoothing, although large numbers have been able to break out of poverty. At the same time the poorest tend not to be reached effectively as microfinance operators have difficulty reaching them.[45] Neither is there any rigorous evidence that the poorest can benefit from microfinance in the sense of being helped out of poverty on a large scale. All evidence seems to indicate that the most important effect of microfinance is to reduce the vulnerability of the poorest and thus make it easier for the poor to master a life in material poverty.

3.6 Christian Microfinance

Christian NGOs were among the institutions pioneering the microfinance movement. Some of the first microfinance projects preceded the celebrated Nobel Prize winner Mohammed Yunus – for example, Mennonite Economic Development Association (MEDA) in Paraguay. Even today

---

45. "Microfinance Operations Have Difficulty Reaching the Very Poor," African Development Bank Group, 1 December 2010, http://www.afdb.org/en/news-and-events/article/microfinance-operations-have-difficulty-reaching-the-very-poor-7548/; accessed 6 May 2011.

one in six microfinance institutions has a link to Christian organizations.[46] On the basis of the discussion in the previous section it may thus be asked whether these general conclusions about microfinance are also valid for Christian microfinance.

3.6.1 Christian Microfinance and Material Poverty Abatement

The first question to be addressed is whether Christian microfinance reaches the poor. There is no available evidence to suggest that the conditions of the loans are much different from those of secular operators. On the other hand, most Christian MFOs tend to work in poor segments of the population in poor countries, whereas the more commercial part of the microfinance industry tends to be located in middle-income countries, and even in OECD countries (e.g. Mexico). Hence the average income of clients of commercial MFOs would be expected to be higher than that of clients of an average Christian MFO. Thus, although there may be a general tendency in microfinance to move up the income ladder, this may not have much significance for Christian MFOs who work in poor segments of the population in poor countries. A number of Christian MFOs that operate on a non-profit basis are able fairly effectively to target client groups which may be expected to be under the poverty lines of USD 1.25 or USD 2 per day. One of the reasons for this is that such MFOs tend to be located in traditional areas of Christian mission, which are mostly poor areas in some of the poorest developing countries in the world, such as Bolivia, Vietnam, Cambodia and Liberia. In such countries large sections of the population live under the poverty line.

Second, it may be asked if Christian microfinance is more successful in helping people to break out of the poverty cycle than MFOs in general. As shown before, general research on microfinance indicates that people are primarily helped to be able to cope with poverty rather than to break out of the poverty trap, the latter being a stated primary objective of Christian microfinance. However, there is no available evidence to conclude that Christian microfinance is more successful in this than others. In order to ensure that a Christian MFO does help the poorest to break out of the poverty cycle in an effective way, the poorest segments of a population would need to

---

46. Roy Mersland, "On the Impact of Religion in the Microfinance Industry: A Multidimensional Comparison of Catholic, Protestant, and Non-religious Microfinance Organizations" (unpublished working paper, University of Agder, Norway, 2010), 3.

be carefully targeted. It would also require the development of loan products which are designed to move people out of poverty.

In order to illustrate the operations and the general performance of Christian microfinance the evaluations of two Christian MFOs may be useful. In an independent assessment of the activities of Diakonia-Frif (D-Frif), a Christian MFO operating in La Paz in Bolivia, the evaluation of results was based mainly on the assessments of the client perception of how their financial and welfare situation had been impacted by the loans from D-Frif.[47] This is a highly subjective approach, but quite illustrative of the kinds of methodological problems encountered in impact studies. In this particular study a comparison was made of the situation ex ante and ex post access to D-Frif loans.

The study concluded that both loans for economic activity (investments) and loans given to microcredit associations (groups of women borrowers) impacted income levels in a favourable way. The major findings were that 91 percent of clients borrowing for economic activity increased their sales and profits following access to the D-Frif loan, and 93 percent of women clients in microcredit associations increased their income following access to D-Frif loans. However, in addition to there not being a control group the study also did not have a base line for income of borrowers, and thus it is not clear what the incomes of the women were prior to obtaining their first loan with D-Frif. Hence, even if it can be shown that the loans had a beneficial impact on their income levels, it is not clear whether the borrowers were already situated above the poverty threshold of USD 1.25 or USD 2 per day, or whether there was a movement within the range or a breaking out of the poverty cycle.

In order to throw some light on complicated incremental income effects from loans, Diakonia-Frif has been able to document a number of real-life stories that illustrate that many do break out of the poverty cycle as a result of microfinance borrowing. There were also a number of other beneficial effects from the inclusion of the women in the microfinance activities: they increased their working capital, the number of people they employed increased, 25 percent of the clients had improved nutrition following access to the loan, and some improved their education and participation in decision making regarding the distribution of household income.[48]

---

47. Profin Foundation, "Study of Impact and Client Satisfaction with the Loan Services of Diaconia-Frif: An Independent Evaluation" (appraisal paper, La Paz, March 2009).
48. Ibid., 63.

There are, however, a large number of Christian MFOs that operate in areas where the whole population in the district tends to be very poor. One study of the microfinance operations in the Mekong Delta carried out by Norwegian Mission Alliance (NMA) in cooperation with the Women's Union in the district is an example.[49] The study was carried out in eight communities in the Mekong Delta and was designed to gain an understanding of livelihood effects after three years of microfinance operations. The research design was based on the methodology of the Livelihood Framework of the UK department for International Development.[50] On average, 35 percent of the clients were considered to fall below the USD 1.25 per day threshold, and the rest tended to be between USD 1.25 and USD 2 per day.

One of the findings was that, since credit from the formal financial sector in the country was not easily accessible in the communities of operation, the microfinance work of NMA led to an increased level of economic activity for the clients, such as in the form of buying a sow, renting a plot of land for rice production or acquiring some electrical equipment for simple furniture production. Second, the financial costs for the clients for the loans were 89 percent lower than if the clients had accessed private moneylenders. The study showed that the social intermediation of the microfinance project enhanced the capacity of the poor to overcome poverty. The group solidarity also provided social networks which could be used in times of difficulty. However, the study could not provide an adequate database for asserting that clients on the whole had experienced an increase in income sufficient to break out of the poverty cycle, but the evidence is quite clear that the microfinance activities improved their capacity to deal with difficult financial situations in their lives – that the loans had the character of consumption smoothing. There are, however, a number of well-documented stories which indicate that an unspecified number of women also moved out of a situation of poverty and improved the welfare of their families through setting up their own production facilities in agriculture, furniture production, and so on, as well as in trading operations.

It may be argued that consumption smoothing in itself has sufficiently beneficial effects to justify Christian social action involvement. If consumption

---

49. "Understanding Beneficiaries Livelihood of Norwegian Mission Alliance's Micro Finance Program in the Tien Giang Province, Mekong Delta Vietnam," Centre for Research Development & Technology Transfer, Bin Duong University, Binh Duong, December 2006.

50. Provention Consortium, http://www.proventionconsortium.org/themes/default/pdfs/tools_for_mainstreaming_GN10.pdf; accessed 5 November 2010.

smoothing is an objective of the MFO, this might be expected to have an effect on its lending strategy. However, there is no evidence available which indicates that Christian MFOs in general take such differentiated strategy objectives into account when designing their financial products.

There is growing evidence that savings services can meet the greatest need among the poor for financial services and that the sole emphasis on credit has been misguided.[51] Poor people have small and irregular incomes. If a person has an average income of USD 1.25 a day, it does not mean that he or she gets it every day. In general poor people are forced to get money for consumption and to cover unexpected events. Hence they need to be money managers as they need both savings and several financial sources to borrow from – be it from friends, relations, NGOs or MFOs – in order to secure their liquidity. Financial services should be available to offer poor people a better way to manage their money and enhance their lifestyle. The one-sided focus on credit products has also led to a lack of mobilization of savings which increases the dependency of Christian MFOs on outside funding sources. In turn this may make the funding of the MFO more expensive and make it difficult to offer credit products at price levels acceptable to the poor. This has become a major concern in the industry.[52]

The Christian community has on the whole been slow to draw conclusions from the research results indicating that the most important effect of microfinance is that it can be an effective instrument in reducing the vulnerability of the poorest and enable them to master their lives in a better way. The websites of Christian microfinance organizations still tend to present microfinance as a powerful instrument for poverty reduction even though available evidence gives scant support for that. For example, the website of Opportunity International says that they "provide small business loans and training so people can work out of poverty with dignity."[53] World Vision states in the same vein: "As we give out loans, lives are changed dramatically."[54]

But what conclusions should Christian MFOs draw from the above findings besides reshaping the text on their websites to reduce the gap between fact and assertions as the whole microfinance industry seems to be

---

51. Dichter and Harper, *What's Wrong with Microfinance?*, 17.

52. Roy Mersland, "The Governance of Non-Profit Micro Finance Institutions: Lessons from History," University of Agder, 6 October 2009, SpringerLink, www.Springerlink.com/index/256132t07065267x.pdf, 5; accessed 10 October 2010.

53. Opportunity International, www.opportunity.org/; accessed 27 March 2010.

54. World Vision, www.wvi.org/; accessed 27 March 2010.

perpetuating the message that microfinance can eradicate poverty on a large scale? Quite clearly more emphasis needs to be placed on what the MFOs can do for the poor by reducing their vulnerability. Microfinance gives access to finance to meet urgent needs that is vital to the lives of poor families and helps them to cope with poverty. As discussed previously, being poor is not only a matter of low income, but also of income that is uneven and vulnerable to disruption.

Furthermore, it seems important to stress the favourable effect of microfinance on female empowerment. As many Christian MFOs have a clear majority of women borrowers, this may have the effect of empowering women socially in their communities. That there is a need for microfinance among the poor is seen most clearly in the way they "vote with their feet." When microfinance is offered to people in a new environment that has previously been excluded from microfinance, people come "out of the woodwork in droves."[55]

The conclusion so far is that Christian MFOs tend to deliver a social good to the poor, but the next question is whether this can be done while maintaining an integral mission perspective which includes spiritual transformation through the proclamation of the gospel.

3.6.2 Targeting Holistic Impact and Proclamation

As discussed above, a Christian holistic understanding of poverty includes spiritual poverty which might be mitigated by the proclamation of the gospel. It is, however, important to note that most development analysts leave out the spiritual dimension as a part of a multifaceted understanding of poverty as their focus tends to be on material poverty abatement.

The issue of structuring microfinance programs to include a spiritual dimension is complex, and measuring spiritual poverty reduction is even more complex. There is quite clearly a tension between the objective of reaching the target group with financial services and at the same time providing a broader range of holistic services by some named spiritual transformation strategies.[56] Thus the specific objectives of the MFO itself will tend to shape the final product strategy of the organization. A perspective on poverty reduction that takes into account the need for a broad perspective on holistic services to the

---

55. Rosenberg, "Does Microcredit Really Help Poor People?", 2.
56. E.g. Bussau and Mask, *Christian Microenterprise Development*, 65.

poor will result in different MFO programs and service designs from those of MFOs which focus narrowly on financial services to reduce poverty as defined in terms of average income per household or on reduction in vulnerability.

Furthermore, the implication of a framework for poverty reduction as contended by Myers means that, in order to bring about lasting changes in the situation of the poor, the broken relationships between the oppressor and the victim also need to be addressed.[57] Hence Myers argues that as only Jesus Christ can bring about a restoration in these interpersonal relationships, Christian development work must also include a clear presentation of the gospel. If this is denied it follows that there will be no real solution to the fundamental causes of poverty. Bussau and Mask argue in the same vein that the Christian MFO should have a deliberate plan and should train personnel in holistic vision, enabling them to integrate spiritual ministries into their daily work routines.[58] However, the major obstacle in arriving at an understanding of how well Christian MFOs perform in relation to holistic services is the lack of data in this area, and that there is no generally accepted method of measurement of holistic impact.

3.6.3 Measuring Holistic Impact and Proclamation

There are no indications that Christian MFOs are less exposed to market pressures than other MFOs. One particular challenge for the Christian MFO is therefore that the market pressures in the microfinance industry may directly impact the ability of a Christian MFO to focus on the reduction of spiritual poverty in the context of Christian integral mission. If this leads to a neglect of holistic mission objectives it reduces the additional value that a Christian MFO represents in the microfinance market. It also undermines the *raison d'être* of the participation of Christian MFOs in the gradually more competitive microfinance market. In many of the prevailing competitive markets it is to be expected that an MFO that leaves will soon be replaced by others. Hence it is doubtful whether the Christian MFOs represent any additional value in comparison with secular operators *at the level of product delivery*, particularly in competitive markets. Christian MFOs can, however, introduce additional value in microfinance operations at the level of product delivery by introducing elements that protect the poor from defaulting on

---

57. Myers, *Walking with the Poor*, 88.
58. Bussau and Mask, *Christian Microenterprise Development*, 66.

loans. The poorest pockets of the populations in poor countries need other antipoverty instruments to enable them to reach a position where they are able to service a microloan. Such instruments may be instruction in basic business techniques and simple bookkeeping, and instruction in the kinds of operations that are planned – for example, fishing, husbandry or wood carving.

The real significance and *raison d'être* of Christian microfinance, however, would have to be found in the holistic aspects which Christian MFOs include in their programs. If holistic aspects are not integrated with the product delivery system of a Christian MFO it might be legitimate to question the significance of its involvement in the microfinance industry.

Mission drift in the area of holistic transformation may be indicated in different ways. The preferred approach would be to have an accurate account of the behaviour of Christian MFOs in relation to integral mission. Unfortunately such data cannot be extracted from a database, and most available data is only available in anecdotal form which may not yield a true picture of the situation. However, it is indicative to study the vision and strategy statements of some of the major operators and to consider a selection of Christian MFOs to gauge the general trend and size of the problem.

In some sense Christian MFOs may be expected to bear a resemblance to entrepreneurial "kingdom companies" which seem to aim specifically at church growth and which tend to link up with the church in its overall mission activities. Kingdom companies aim specifically at church growth but integrated in overall mission activities and operated on biblical principles to impact society in a favourable way and attempt to influence individuals for Christ. These efforts are said to have given remarkable results.[59]

As in the secular microfinance market Christian MFOs detail in their mission statements what they want to achieve through their operations: poverty reduction, gender equality, improved education and health, and so on. It is evident that mission drift is likely if the objectives and values in the vision statements are not transformed into a strategy that may be realistically implemented. Some Christian MFOs include certain holistic objectives, thus reflecting an integral mission approach to microfinance, whereas others are more general in their vision and strategy formulations. The three MFOs listed below as examples are among the biggest Christian MFOs. They are all

---

59. Tetsunao Yamamori and Kenneth A. Eldred, *On Kingdom Business: Transforming Missions through Entrepreneurial Strategies* (Wheaton: Crossway, 2007), 197.

private non-profit organizations, and some of them get large donations from private and public donors. Key quotations from their mission statements are reproduced in order to throw some light on their commitment to integral mission objectives and the abatement of spiritual poverty:

HOPE International

HOPE International (HOPE) is a Christian faith-based . . . non-profit organization focused on alleviating physical and spiritual poverty through micro-enterprise development . . .

But HOPE isn't only concerned with physical poverty. Christ-following loan officers share the hope of the Gospel in the context of relationships, ministering to spiritual poverty as well.[60]

Opportunity International

Our vision is a world in which all people have the opportunity to provide for their families and build a fulfilling life.

Our belief is that small-scale entrepreneurs can be big change agents in overcoming global poverty.

Our mission is to empower people to work their way out of chronic poverty, transforming their lives, their children's future and their communities.

Our method is to provide microfinance services, including lending, saving and transformation training to people in need. To this we build and work through sustainable, local microfinance institutions.

Our motivation is to respond to Jesus Christ's call to love and serve the poor.

Our motivation: Opportunity International heeds Christ's call to serve the poor by providing opportunities for impoverished people to transform their lives through micro-enterprise development, providing small business loans and training so people can work out of poverty with dignity. This strategy

---

60. HOPE International, http://www.hopeinternational.org/about-hope/; accessed 27 March 2010.

demonstrates God's concern for the poor is not just to meet their economic needs, but to empower them to meet their own needs.[61]

World Relief

The Vision: In community with the local church, World Relief envisions the most vulnerable people transformed economically, socially and spiritually.

Values: The local church as a primary agent of bringing peace, justice and love to a broken world. The integrated "word" and "deed" dimensions of God's mandate, as evidenced through the church's integral, or transformational, mission are necessary to bringing reconciliation and restoration to God, others and the environment.[62]

Both HOPE and World Relief have clear references to abatement of spiritual poverty and present a clear integral mission profile, although HOPE is considerably more explicit than World Relief, particularly with respect to the proclamation part of integral mission. In the case of Opportunity International (OI) the mission statement has no clear reference that might indicate a commitment to integral mission objectives. The statement is full of vague phrases about the motivation of love and a strong belief in their ability to transform people's lives through micro-enterprise development and product delivery mechanisms. On the basis of its mission statement OI may be expected to have some mission drift.

The present mission statement of OI is a far cry from the aspirations of David Bussau, one of its founders and sometimes called the father of Christian microfinance, and Russell Mask, who together wrote in 2003: "To ensure that all development work, including MED[63] and microfinance, become explicit partners in evangelism, stimulate conversion to Christ, enable growth and discipleship, and strengthen the local church, it is essential that

---

61. International Opportunity, http://www.opportunity.org/; accessed 27 March 2010.

62. World Relief, http://worldrelief.org/mission-vision; accessed 27 March 2010.

63. MED is an abbreviation for micro-enterprise development and Christian micro-enterprise development is an integrated, holistic Christian approach to microfinance. Bussau and Mask, *Christian Microenterprise Development*, 3.

the five preceding attributes[64] of Christian MED should be made explicit in organizational vision and mission statements."[65] This statement would make the objective of OI quite similar to that expressed in the mission statements of "kingdom companies" as described above.

The reason for the indicated possible mission drift in OI may be explained by the impact of some or all of the key drivers discussed below which over time may weaken the ability of a Christian MFO to deliver results in spiritual poverty abatement. It has professionalized the organization and is extensively funded by secular organizations, among them the Bill Gates Foundation. To the extent that the mission drift in relation to integral mission is as serious as it would appear from its mission statement the operations of OI might probably be basically indistinguishable from non-Christian MFOs engaged in microfinance with the objective to reduce material and social poverty.

The mission statements may, however, have limited value with respect to reflecting accurately what is actually happening in the field. It would be expected that a Christian MFO would have its supporters and sponsors in view when formulating its vision and value statements. Thus an MFO that sources its funding from evangelical churches may stress the evangelistic element in its mission statement, whereas a Christian MFO with a predominantly secular funding base may be tempted to downplay the proclamation part of the activities, even if it exists.

3.6.4 Key Drivers for Mission Drift in Relation to Proclamation

There are indications that Christian microfinance enterprises find it increasingly difficult to maintain the proclamation part of integral mission objectives. There are several reasons for this. In the following are described the key drivers for mission drift that may be likely to impact the ability of a Christian MFO to deliver results in relation to proclamation.

First, high growth requires increased external funding. The markets for microfinance products are increasingly competitive, requiring high

---

64. The five preceding attributes of "Christian" development which serve as a guide to review vision and mission of MED are, first, does the vision support the belief in the necessity for a personal relationship to Jesus Christ? Second, does the vision contend that Christian development must have its foundations in a biblical worldview? Third, does Christian development include the church (both global and local)? Fourth, does the mission include work for the holistic development of people? And finally, does the mission reflect an understanding of the multi-dimensional nature of deprivation?

65. Bussau and Mask, *Christian Microenterprise Development*, 7.

efficiency and a low cost level for the MFOs to survive. This is evidenced by the remarkable growth of MFOs in many markets. The high growth in the microfinance market requires a steady inflow of funds to underpin the capital base of an MFO. These funds would normally be secured from public funds (e.g. government budgets for development cooperation) or from large secular sponsors that are inclined not to support MFOs that have an evangelism component on their agenda. In other words, these sponsors require not only high efficiency and high outreach numbers, but also that elements of proclamation should not be supported by their financing of the enterprise. The major multilateral financing banks, the United Nations and bilateral governmental international development agencies do not accept the use of their funds in what is called proselytism.

Second, there is substantial pressure for financial sustainability. As MFOs aim at financially sustainable operations in an increasingly competitive market this makes it gradually more difficult for MFO staff to engage in holistic activities, including evangelism and discipleship training. In the early stages of the development of microfinance this was not a practical limitation. In the current environment Christian MFOs have to maintain efficient operations and secure competitive funding in order to survive as sustainable financial entities. The challenge before Christian MFOs as they are faced with the requirement to keep the costs of loan delivery low is that this reduces the relationship between the loan officers and the clients to an economic transaction making holistic transformation work less likely.

In such an environment it is thus increasingly more difficult to maintain the objective of spiritual poverty abatement. Primarily services will be provided that clients can and are willing to pay for out of their cash flow. This does not mean that spiritual transformation has to be left aside as Christian sponsors may be requested to meet the costs of carrying out spiritual transformation activities. However, as much of the funding of the financial operations of the enterprise comes from sources that do not accept evangelistic components this option may not be pursued. Even if that should be possible, the sheer size of some of the operations is such that these donations would have to be sizeable for Christian donors to be able to provide "sufficient funds to keep the 'word' and 'deed' aspects of programs in balance."[66] On the other hand,

---

66. Brian Fikkert, "Christian Microfinance: Which Way Now?", paper prepared for the Association of Christian Economists 20th Anniversary Conference, 5–6 January 2003. Chalmers University. Accessed 21 February 2010, www.chalmers.org/resources/documents/ workingpaper205.pdf.

if the Christian MFOs actively partner with local churches this may leverage the capacity of the organizations for evangelism and discipleship services.[67] Traditionally MFOs have been reluctant to engage in such cooperation with local churches for a number of reasons, particularly as some MFOs are afraid that if the operations are too closely linked to a church it will result in repayment problems in cases of payment default.[68] This implies that for some MFOs concerns about financial survival take precedence over biblical principles and holistic transformation.

Third, the rapid growth of microfinance organizations tends to put pressure on recruitment as there seems to be a continuous need to provide more credit officers and at times personnel with higher levels of professionalism than the NGO or church organization is able to provide from its own human resource base. This in turn makes it challenging for a Christian MFO to maintain the same level of adherence to its core values at the operational level. Microfinance is labour intensive. One credit officer may be able to service anything from 250 to 800 clients, and credit officers must be locals speaking the language of the clients. When MFOs increase to tens of thousands or hundreds of thousands of clients, the MFO feels forced to hire staff who do not necessarily share the value basis of the organization. This trend is reinforced by increased regulatory requirements for the microfinance industry as a whole, which increases the need for professional staff who may not be able to share the holistic value base of the organization.

As Christian microfinance has moved from being NGO projects to formalized MFOs, it is to be expected that difficult issues related to maintaining the core values of a Christian organization will have emerged. A major challenge for Christian MFOs as they grow larger is therefore how holistic mission objectives may be preserved.

Fourth, if the trends of thinking in Christian integral mission circles tend to place less emphasis on the proclamation aspects of integral mission this may impact the top management thinking of Christian MFOs and subsequently weaken the focus on the spiritual poverty abatement aspect of their operations.

Fifth, microfinance operations tend to take place in the context of a professional and cultural situation where biblical assumptions are not shared by the community in which the social action program is located. Social action

---

67. Ibid., 21.
68. Bussau and Mask, *Christian Microenterprise Development*, 13.

in Christian mission in such circumstances is now not uncommonly almost dissociated from evangelism, and rather identified as a social service to the community, ethical pronouncement and political involvement.[69]

It follows from the last point that there may be a lack of proclamation simply because the cultural environment is not sympathetic to the Christian faith and the Christian worker finds it a challenge to communicate the gospel. Yet in other instances it may be some kind of combination of the two previous points – both a lack of conviction as to the content of the integral mission mandate and a lack of cultural courage or ability to communicate effectively – that deters the church worker from evangelism. Little has been written to clarify whether this is the situation in integral mission activities and, if so, how it may be rectified. One reason may be that it is simply taken for granted that the proclamation of the gospel will flow naturally from the believers or that the church does not put enough effort into the planning and preparation of the evangelism part of the mission mandate in social action programs. It may also be that in many situations it is easier to concentrate on that part of the integral mission mandate that gives social recognition and to leave aside the integral mission requirement to proclaim the gospel.

The final affirmation at the Manila conference pledges to study the society in which the church lives and operates in order to understand its structures, values and needs, "and so develop an appropriate strategy of mission."[70] If this is implemented it may bring about a change and make evangelism a close ally of social action. This is not the place to attempt a broad-based analysis of the culture(s) in which the church operates; suffice it to say that in the postmodern cultural climate of the West an aggressive absolutism has emerged that is quite intolerant of anyone asserting that there is a universal truth. In this culture of relativism the Christian communicator must be able to contextualize the Christian message so that the listener is able to understand what is communicated. This requires courage and hard work, but it is not something new for the church. Even during the times of persecution of early Christians some took up the defence of the Christian faith and a number of works were published in defence of Christianity.[71]

---

69. Andrew Kirk, *Mission Under Scrutiny: Considering Current Challenges* (London: Darton, Longman & Todd, 2006), 47.

70. Lausanne Movement, "Manila Manifesto," Affirmation 18, http://www.lausanne.org/content/manifesto/the-manila-manifesto; accessed 9 November 2010.

71. F. F. Bruce, *The Spreading Flame* (Exeter: Paternoster, 1982), 176.

Neither is it new that the influence of prevailing philosophies impairs the thinking of Christians inside the churches. In the early church the threat came not only from the outside but also from inside the church, as many Christians were influenced by Greek thinking and Gnosticism that had the effect of toning down the content of the gospel. Paul addresses this issue in his letter to the Corinthians. In the church in Corinth the *sophia* (wisdom) of the mainly Greek members of the church[72] may have been influenced not only by incipient Gnosticism,[73] but also by the Platonic view that the body and the spirit are separated from each other. In contrast Paul speaks of their unity.[74]

The church is thus not immune from the impact of external philosophical influences. Bosch argues that the impact of many of the Gnostic elements penetrated the church so deeply that they can be felt even today, and that the struggle against Gnosticism was so severe that the church had to forfeit its opportunity for rapid growth and rather clarify and consolidate its teaching on theological issues.[75]

The contemporary church may benefit in its integral mission undertakings from a practical approach to contextualization. The most challenging task for the contemporary church may be that of making the gospel understandable to people who no longer share the presuppositions of Christianity and the methodology of how we approach the issues of truth and knowing.[76] In order to structure and lead church-based integral mission programs that also honour the mandate to evangelize, it is essential to understand the context of the pressure of contemporary pluralism, relativism and theological universalism. It is increasingly challenging and demanding for a Christian worker to proclaim Christ as the incarnation of God and the only way to salvation. This may have a psychological influence on the proclamation part. To defend the proclamation leg of integral mission in this context is a demanding undertaking and one which has not been given much attention in integral mission literature. Up until now writers on integral mission seem to have been more concerned to show how important an integral mission perspective is than to confront the demands on individual Christians in the field.

---

72. G. D. Fee, *The First Epistle to the Corinthians* (NICNT; Grand Rapids: Eerdmans, 1987), 10.

73. F. F. Bruce, *Paul: Apostle of the Free Spirit* (Carlisle: Paternoster, 1995), 261.

74. E.g. 1 Cor 6:19–20.

75. Bosch, *Transforming Mission*, 200.

76. F. Schaeffer, *Trilogy: The God Who Is There; Escape from Reason; He Is There and He Is Not Silent* (Wheaton: Crossway, 1990), 6.

However, "cultural plurality is nothing new for Christian mission," says C. J. H. Wright, who continues: "it is rather the very stuff of missional engagement and missiological reflection. We may be challenged by swimming in the postmodern pool, but we may not feel out of our depth there."[77] He refers to a survey by Andrew F. Walls that illustrates how the Christian church has developed an ever-growing pluriformity as it has taken root in culture after culture while preserving the essential non-negotiable and trans-cultural objective core of the gospel.[78]

The history of missiology is a history of the church learning more about the impact of culture on Christian mission. There are thus a number of factors in social communities that may make it difficult for the church to master the evangelistic mandate in Christian social action as well as in other areas of the work of the church.

3.7 Conclusion

The biblical understanding of poverty which includes spiritual poverty has far-reaching consequences for the strategy of Christian microfinance organizations. Poverty abatement strategies should be multifaceted, holistic, and integrate both a strategy for the abatement of economic poverty as well as a spiritual transformation strategy involving the proclamation of the gospel of salvation and release.

This chapter has shown that Christian microfinance organizations are confronted with several mission drift drivers in relation to Christian integral mission objectives. The most serious drivers of mission drift tend to be generated by high-volume growth, recruitment policies, the need for long-term financial sustainability, misinterpretation of the integral mission concept and the need to ensure external funding from agencies that make funding conditional upon non-proclamation of the gospel. The risk for mission drift in Christian MFOs tends to be more serious in relation to the proclamation part of Christian integral mission than in relation to the delivery of a social good to the poor. The main reason for this is that Christian MFOs tend to target poor people, although most of the lending does not have income effects of such magnitude that people break out of the poverty trap.

---

77. Wright, *The Mission of God*, 46.
78. Ibid., 46.

The lending nevertheless has the effect of consumption smoothing, which in itself is beneficial and important for poor households.

Although mission drift in relation to spiritual transformation is difficult to measure, the increased commercialization of microfinance makes it difficult for Christian MFOs to cope with the extra costs and the demand on human resources that a holistic and spiritual transformation strategy entails. This in turn might result in mission drift in relation to holistic objectives. The trend toward professionally run Christian MFOs without emphasis on spiritual transformation strategies to combat spiritual poverty may also creep into vision and strategy statements.

The situation is serious in the sense that the holistic mission objectives which Christian MFOs initially set out to reach are threatened. To the extent that this is true it would not be easy to detect a significant difference between a Christian MFO and secular MFO operators that base their operations on general development objectives to help the poor.

For Christian MFOs to ensure that they operate in a way which is compatible with integral mission-based social action as discussed in chapter 2, new and creative planning mechanisms and techniques may be required. If it is possible to *anticipate* that microfinance as social action will constitute a platform to communicate the gospel in a local community and thus lead to spiritual transformation, there may be a need to take the drivers of mission drift into account at an early stage in the practical planning of Christian microfinance operations. Some key questions are related to the financing of the costs of holistic services in the Christian MFOs, the recruitment policies, general funding policies and the role of the local church in the community of operation. It is not unthinkable that outside resources may be brought in to take care of the holistic aspects in relation to the MFO operations. Without there being a clear element of verbal proclamation in the execution of Christian MFO operations, the operations may provide useful social assistance, but it is not Christian mission as defined by the evangelical community taking part in the Lausanne process.

Given the serious pressures toward mission drift in Christian microfinance, one might rightly ask if microfinance can be a viable platform for integral mission. In other words, are there Christian MFOs that have succeeded in serving the poor and employing microfinance as a platform for evangelism and yet are financially viable? If such an MFO could be identified this in itself would represent an empirical piece of evidence that it is possible to employ microfinance as a platform for Christian integral mission. In addition, if a successful model for microfinance as integral mission exists, it would be useful to learn what has enabled such an MFO to steer away from the dangers of mission drift. This is the purpose of the next chapter.

4

The Viability of Microfinance as a Platform for Christian Integral Mission

In this chapter I report the results of a field study that was carried out in order to establish whether it is feasible for a Christian microfinance organization to combine the demands of integral mission and incorporate both the delivery of a social good for the poor and evangelism. Given the risks of mission drift in the areas of product delivery, target groups and spiritual transformation, as outlined in the previous chapter, the most obvious way for a Christian MFO to maintain an integral mission operation would be to address the risk factors listed in that chapter. I would expect Christian MFOs that do address these risks in a serious manner to be less impacted by mission drift in relation to product delivery and proclamation than those organizations that do not deal with these risks.

In order to clarify whether microfinance may constitute a viable vehicle for Christian integral mission, I decided to make field studies in the Philippines and Thailand. The Philippine operation that was studied, the Centre for Community Transformation (CCT), is fairly large (in 2010 around 130,000 clients) and is located in a country with a highly developed microfinance industry. The Thai microfinance operation, Step Ahead (SA), is quite small (in 2010 around 1,200 clients) and it is located in a country with a less-developed microfinance industry. The Thai study is thus also less comprehensive than that for CCT as there is less activity and fewer products and services.

The two institutions were chosen for closer examination for two main reasons. First, they were referred to by the author of *Christian Microenterprise Development*, David Bussau, as institutions that have endeavoured to integrate product delivery and proclamation of the gospel in their strategic microfinance platform for poverty eradication. Second, they operate in two entirely different cultures, one being predominantly Christian and the other predominantly Buddhist. This would make it possible to consider whether cultural differences impact the success of Christian microfinance operations that are based on an integral mission concept.

There were two rounds of discussions with the management of CCT and SA regarding strategies and operations – the first in October 2010 and the second in February 2011. In addition, a selection of clients of CCT and SA were visited in order to obtain an understanding of the nature of the operations. The field study in the Philippines, four days in all, included discussions with the Microfinance Council of the Philippines (MCP), which is made up of forty-five institutions. MCP's major focus is on both expanding the microfinance network in the country and encouraging member organizations to place an increased emphasis on Social Performance Management (SPM).[1] Discussions were also conducted with the top management of the Alliance of Philippine Partners in Enterprise Development (APPEND). The major part of the field study spent with CCT consisted of discussions with the top management of the organization, site visits to the branches, attending meetings with clients, and viewing operations conducted for the very poor, the street dwellers. During the field visits to Thailand in October 2010 and February 2011, four days in all, I met with both SA management and a number of clients, poor people who have already established some kind of business in quite modest forms.

Notes were taken from the meetings with management personnel and clients in both the Philippines and Thailand, and these form the basis for parts of the text that follows.

Below, CCT and SA are studied separately with special reference to poverty eradication, financial sustainability and evangelism in the context of integral mission objectives and requirements.

4.1 The Philippine Microfinance Industry and the Issue of Mission Drift

The Philippines is a country of near 100 million inhabitants. On the basis of a survey conducted by the National Statistical Coordination Board (NSCB) in 2007 there were 13.8 million families, 4.15 million of whom were considered

---

1. Microfinance Council of the Philippines (MCP), 2009 Annual Report, Manila, 2010, 5.

poor.[2] Thus, over 30 percent of the families were considered to fall below the local poverty threshold. The annual per capita poverty threshold was set by the Philippine government at PHP 11,458 (approximately USD 494) in 2008, or USD 1.3 per day. The Philippines has a robust microfinance industry with three major providers of microfinance services: NGOs, rural banks and cooperatives. It is estimated that there are 1,707 MFOs composed of 300 NGOs, 1,178 cooperatives and 229 rural and cooperative banks.[3] A significant number of the MFOs are members of the Microfinance Council. The sheer size and dynamism of the Philippine microfinance industry is such that it is gradually becoming a part of the formal financial system. The Council also focuses on SPM in microfinance. While stating that MFOs need to maintain an emphasis on growth and financial sustainability, the Council is critical of the fact that their quest for profitability has led many MFOs to drift away from their social mission. Instead of serving those with little or no access to financial services, they have begun to focus on clients who represent lower credit risk, thus excluding really poor people. The Council wants to track MFOs' social mission and how microfinance contributes to positive changes in clients' lives. This initiative has been motivated by discouraging tendencies in the industry: "Competition and the drive for higher rates of return, and increased outreach, have also led to credit pollution in most urban centres and to the over-indebtedness of microfinance clients . . . caused by their failure to understand and respond to their clients' complex needs."[4]

4.1.1 Christian MFOs

It is within this microfinance industry framework that Christian MFOs operate in the Philippines. As becomes clear from the commitment of the Microfinance Council to improve the social performance of MFOs in the country, the objective to serve the poor is not something that characterizes only Christian MFOs. The reality of mission drift in relation to social objectives as stated by the Council is a matter of concern also in relation to MFOs that do not have Christian ownership.

---

2. Philippine Statistics Authority National Statistical Coordination Board (NSCB), projection on the 2007 survey on population, NSCB, http://www.census.gov/ph; accessed 28 October 2010.

3. Ledesma and Davis-Casis, *Mission First*, 7.

4. Ibid., 3.

In the context of a Christian integral mission framework it would be expected that Christian MFOs, in addition to having the double bottom line of financial sustainability and positive social effects for the poor clients, also adopt the third bottom line, that of employing microfinance as a base for Christian holistic ministry that includes spiritual transformation.

Besides having a large and robust microfinance industry, the Philippines is probably the country with the largest Christian microfinance institutions in the world. There are ten Christian MFOs in the Philippines that may be termed major operations, all of which characterize themselves as Christian mission according to their mission statements. Nine of them are members of the APPEND, and the tenth is the CCT. Some of the mission statements of APPEND members are formulated in general terms such as "responding to the call of Christ to serve the poor," which may or may not include proclamation. Others are more clearly formulated, such as "Actively share Christ and promote Christian values."[5]

According to APPEND management, the staff of their member organizations tend to be partly Christian, partly non-Christian. This poses a difficulty in relation to using microfinance as a platform for evangelism for a fast-increasing client base. The main vehicle for sharing the gospel is the credit officers. Without a commitment to the Christian faith it is hard to conceive that credit officers will share the Christian gospel with clients. For the above reasons the nine Christian member organizations of APPEND have met problems when trying to establish a platform for evangelism and they are reported to have varying degrees of success. APPEND had recommended that their member MFOs should use standard study material at weekly client meetings, but APPEND as an advisory body does not have any means of enforcing it. The APPEND study material applies experiences from daily life to spiritual issues, and all credit officers were considered able to use it.[6] Some of the organizations in APPEND had also employed a full-time worker to handle holistic mission issues, but with limited success, as the key to holistic mission in organizations with 100,000 clients or more necessarily lies with a dedicated credit officer group.

The focus of these organizations tends to be on credit development, and holistic issues are one aspect that they would like to incorporate as an

---

5. KMBI, http:www.kmbi.org.ph/index.php?option=com_content&view=article&id=98&Ite mi; accessed 28 September 2010.

6. Alliance of Philippine Partners in Enterprise Development Incorporated (APPEND), *Household Chores* (Manila: Timotheos Publishing, 2008).

additional activity in their operations – but so far this has been achieved with limited success. Poverty eradication, increased outreach and credit growth seem to constitute the primary objectives of their operations. The CCT, which was selected for a closer study, did have a mission profile that was distinctly different from the others from an integral mission point of view. In CCT, spiritual transformation processes were integrated into the microfinance operations.

4.1.2 The Centre for Community Transformation (CCT)

The microfinance operations of CCT started in 1992. The founders were "convinced that relationship with God is the starting point and sustaining power in the true transformation of individuals, families and communities."[7] In 2003 the microfinance operations were transformed into a Credit Cooperative and registered with the Philippine Securities and Exchange Commission. From the start CCT clearly conceived of itself as a mission organization in a way which was in line with integral mission theology. CCT states that it is a Christian social action response to poverty and social injustice. "It serves urban and rural communities throughout the Philippines in pursuit of its desire to see changed lives, strong families and transformed communities centred on the Lordship of Jesus Christ," and the goal "is that at least 5% of the communities we serve are followers of Jesus Christ and agents of transformation."[8] At an early stage in the meetings with CCT the organization expressed a determination to address mechanisms that tend to produce mission drift, such as personnel policies, funding strategies, and high growth with a lopsided focus on profitability at the expense of spiritual transformation strategies. It would be expected that mission drift in relation to spiritual transformation will be less in such an organization than in those which have not addressed these mechanisms.

The main difference between the operations of CCT and the other organizations in the sample is at the level of vision and strategy. A distinctive feature of CCT is that it integrates microfinance into its transformational programs and services for the poor. In order to facilitate this process, the programs offered by CCT for the communities integrate the efforts to eradicate

---

7. CCT Group of Ministries, "Organizational Primer" (Undated, unpublished in-house document, Manila), 4.

8. MPC 2009 Annual Report, 5. CCT, *Serving Like Jesus: Yearbook 2009* (Manila: CCT Group of Ministries, 2010), 1.

poverty with evangelism and discipleship training. CCT thus considers its microfinance activities as a vehicle for mission as well as a vehicle for poverty eradication, and the mission vision underpins the activities. These consist of two equally important arms: the product delivery/poverty eradication activities, and spiritual transformation/evangelism activities. The spiritual transformation process is anchored on a twin strategy of evangelism and discipleship.[9] The discipleship part addresses the continued formation of the values and priorities of the community partners, the leaders and the staff.

The findings indicate that the main difference between CCT and the nine Christian MFOs in APPEND is that CCT has spiritual transformation strategies for its microfinance operations which are clearly Christian-mission driven, whereas the others may be characterized as organizations having Christian ownership but with their main focus being on microfinance transactions for poverty eradication. Microfinance is about transactions. Spiritual transformation is about relationships. In integral mission, the two areas demand a coordinated response.

4.1.3 The Operational Framework of the CCT and Financial Sustainability

CCT had 131,569 partners (clients) at year end 2010 and is one of the major Christian MFOs in the Philippines. It has operations in 11 regions, 23 provinces, 49 cities and 42 municipalities. There are 133 community-based branches overseen by 339 loan officers-cum-covenant-community builders. CCT practises individual lending with group guarantees. CCT Credit Cooperative is owned by the clients, called "partners" in CCT. There are 2,000 full members with a varying number of shares, and approximately 130,000 associate members, each with a minimum shareholding of one share worth PHP 50 (approximately USD 1.25). Credit cooperatives are allowed to collect savings from their members and are regulated and supervised by the government agency Cooperative Development Authority. All partners are "associated partners" with the exception of those who are accepted as full partners and co-owners of the CCT Credit Cooperative with voting rights.[10] Besides offering loans and savings products, the cooperative also offers micro-insurance for its members.

---

9. CCT, "Organizational Primer," 9.
10. CCT, *Serving Like Jesus*, 1.

Both the board and the daily operations of CCT are managed by professionals with many years of experience in social action and management.[11] CCT is also a Tearfund partner in the Philippines. The pricing policies of CCT are in line with normal microfinance practice in the country, with varying interest levels depending on the type of market segment.

On 31 December 2010 the total assets of the CCT Credit Cooperative were approximately PHP 496 million (around USD 14.2 million; 1 USD = PHP 43.4). Net taxable surplus from operations is low by microfinance standards with a 0.5 percent return on average total assets (ROA) and a mere 2.5 percent return on equity (ROE). The liquidity situation is healthy, with a current ratio (current assets in relation to current liabilities) of 2.0.[12] However, when considering these figures it is important to be aware that the Philippine tax regulations are quite liberal with respect to the assessment of some key cost items (e.g. loan loss provisions, estimated social service provisions), and this tends to colour the financial statements with the effect that estimates of the profitability of the operations are lower than they would otherwise be.

The company has an adequate capital structure with an equity share of total capital of 20.6 percent and a satisfactory asset quality. The real debt service is reported to be satisfactory with a portfolio at risk over 1 day of 6.8 percent, which increased in 2010 due to the financial crises which have also affected the Philippine economy.

The overall financial performance of CCT implies that to the extent that CCT is successful in integral mission this has not jeopardized its long-term financial sustainability. Thus it may be concluded that CCT is able to deliver on the first bottom line for Christian microfinance, namely, ensuring that the operations are financially sustainable.

4.1.4 Target Groups and Poverty Eradication

In addition to microfinance, the total ministry of CCT covers a number of social action arenas: education, family and community health care, social security and natural disaster response.

---

11. The president and cofounder of CCT is Ruth Callanta, a well-known social action activist in the Philippines. She has worked with Asian Development Bank and UN agencies and has extensive experience in development issues. The president of the board is Bertram Lim, an MIT graduate.

12. The ratios are calculated on the basis of figures in the Financial Statement for the years ended 31 December 2010 and 2009 auditors report (Ms Mary Ann R. Dela Pena, Certified Public Accountant).

The microfinance ministry for poverty eradication was structured in a pyramid form with measures to improve the lives of the poorest (street dwellers) forming the base. The next target group is termed "rank and file factory workers," followed by the last pyramid layer: micro-entrepreneurs. The CCT objective is to move the two lowest group layers up to the micro-entrepreneur level, and finally to move all out of poverty.

The street dwellers need long-term livelihood assistance, education and health services. CCT addresses tough issues such as drug use, illiteracy and corruption, all of which ensnare the poorest. The street dwellers do not receive loans, but CCT helps them to survive and actively assists them to move out of dire poverty to the next level, where they may obtain a paid job.

The factory worker category is not considered among the poorest inasmuch as their employers would normally comply with labour laws. However, they receive only a minimum daily salary for the maintenance of their often large families. A substantial part of the urban population is therefore under severe financial pressure to close the gap between income and expenditure and they find ways of coping with their needs by means of after-work self-employment occupations, advance wage payments from employers and loans from usurious moneylenders. For this group CCT extends livelihood loans for consumption smoothing.

The objective of CCT is to move some of these clients toward the micro-entrepreneur stage through vocational training. Micro-enterprises are defined as businesses that employ fewer than five people and provide the sole source of family income or other supplemental form of income. It is estimated that about 4.1 million Filipino families in the lowest income strata are engaged in a wide range of micro-enterprise activities such as fruit sales, tiny street shops and street food-serving facilities with a simple table or two.[13] They lack assets for collateral and are registered as self-employed in the informal sector. As they have no collateral, in the absence of MFO services they are forced to turn to moneylenders, which in turn weakens their chance to grow their business due to the exorbitant pricing of loans.

For each of these groups of poor people CCT has designed products that may improve their living standards and finally assist them to break out of the poverty cycle. Efforts are made to achieve synergies between the different ministries in CCT. Thus street dwellers do not get loans at that stage, but rather they get subsistence gifts and educational support so that they are able

---

13. CCT, *Serving Like Jesus*, 30.

to move onto the next level in the CCT pyramid where they may get a rank and file worker job. Thereby the poorest are also included in and financed by the microfinance operations. The pyramid structure of CCT target groups is useful in avoiding mission drift at the level of product delivery and target group. The average loan outstanding is approximately PHP 3,263 or USD 75.2, which indicates that CCT targets poor groups in the population.

It may be concluded that CCT has a strong poverty eradication focus, a significant outreach among the poor and solid results in this area. Thus it may be concluded that CCT is able to deliver on the second bottom line of Christian microfinance, that of delivering a socially beneficial service to the poor.

4.1.5 Holistic Mission and Spiritual Transformation

The basic design of the CCT operational model is that its social action program for poverty eradication constitutes a holistic platform for evangelism. Thus the management of CCT does not consider CCT as primarily a microfinance organization. The CCT Transformational Development Framework (TDF) consists of two main parts, a process and a program, which are interlinked.[14] The TDF is designed to ensure that the operations are integrated, holistic and transformational.

The process part includes the spiritual transformation process at the individual level. A new Christian believer is introduced to a new perspective and worldview which in turn impacts values, priorities and decision making. The process to encourage a person's spiritual growth is taken care of by the Spiritual Development ministry. This ministry incorporates program evangelism and discipleship training, which are designed to result in changed lives.

The CCT programs in the areas of microfinance, education, health care, insurance and fellowship groups are designed to meet the material needs of a person by improving the income level, the social situation and the social capital base.[15] On the basis of an improved quality of life of the individual, material and spiritual transformation programs are developed with a view to strengthening the family units of the partners. This may in turn have overall positive impacts on community life. The various programs of the TDF

---

14. Ruth S. Callanta, *A Transformational Strategy* (Manila: CCT, 2009), 6.
15. Primarily through the interaction of partners in fellowship groups.

framework in microfinance, education, leadership and the strengthening of value systems are thus structured in a way that may ensure important synergies between the programs that meet material needs and those that meet spiritual needs and which may culminate in community transformation.

The role of the church is important in CCT. Pastors from various evangelical denominations are involved in the spiritual transformation program in all parts of the country. However, the pastors are not allowed to invite partners to their own churches. Choice of church is left with the individual partner in each group to decide. Initially CCT tried to channel the microfinance operations, lending and collecting, through churches. However, this was not a success. The main reason for the lack of success was that the discipline of microfinance was not compatible with the thinking and sentiment of the church. The collection part of microfinance becomes difficult when pastors must collect and enforce payments from members of their own churches. Yet the collection phase is crucial for the survival of a microfinance institution. New churches are formed when many become Christians in one geographical area as a result of the CCT work. This may happen if there is no local church in the area or if CCT management in consultation with the partners finds that the existing local church might not be adequately equipped to cope with the demands of discipleship training for new Christians.

A feature of key importance in CCT is that *all* employees are professing evangelical Christians in the same way as a mission board traditionally would not employ non-Christians to communicate the gospel. In 2003 there was a growing awareness on the board and at top management level of the need for a change of approach for the microfinance organization to have a spiritual transformation impact in the communities that were served. The change thus started at the top, with the board in turn discipling the senior staff, preparing them for operating a continued program for evangelism and discipleship that was launched in 2004. At the same time the microfinance program was growing rapidly in volume. The organizational terminology was changed. Clients became partners. Weekly business meetings became partner meetings with a substantial Bible teaching element. Group leaders became team servants; area managers became community servants.

At CCT poverty eradication and spiritual transformation are operationally integrated. New clients (formally "associated" partners, but now simply "partners") are included in the partner groups. A partner takes on an individual loan, but the group guarantees correct repayment in the case of default. Each new partner has to be recommended by two other members of the group in order to be able to join. In the event of a default of a loan by an individual borrower, the repayment is made by the whole group. Thus the group wants to make sure that new partners are in a position to repay.

One key feature of CCT operations is that there is full transparency with respect to partnership. New partners are informed at the outset that there is also a spiritual transformation aspect to a partnership in addition to the economic one. Once a week there is a partner meeting that starts with a spiritual session in which there is teaching from the Bible, and this is followed by a business session in which the transaction is reviewed. The competition between MFOs in the Philippines is high; hence a person who does not wish to be a part of the spiritual transformation process may easily obtain a loan elsewhere.

In spite of this obligatory requirement to come to the weekly partner meetings as a part of a spiritual transformation process, the growth of CCT was so rapid that in 2008 the board decided to slow down the partner growth as it was felt that the spiritual transformation part could not keep up with such rapid numerical expansion. For this reason the number of CCT partners was kept between 130,000 and 140,000 up till the end of 2010. At the start of 2011 the board considered that the necessary capacity was in place for further numerical expansion.

Many find it attractive and interesting to attend the weekly Bible studies. Some Muslims attend, and as nobody is asked to convert but only to attend the studies, this is socially accepted in the cultural setting of the Philippines. Most of the partners, however, have a Roman Catholic background and would tend to be familiar with Christian prayer and worship.

4.1.6 Performance and Results

In contemporary development thinking, performance and specific measurable results rather than size of activities has become the key parameter for assessing the achievements and the efficiency of a development project. CCT has extended this to the area of measuring spiritual transformation effects. It may be argued that the measurement of effects in this area is important because integral mission strategies will be lacking if results are produced only in the areas of finance and product delivery. Holistic transformation also requires the third bottom line, that of the spiritual transformation of the individual. The process of putting numbers on spiritual transformation is not unknown in the Christian church. Thus we read in Acts 4:4 that "many of those who heard the word believed, and the number of the men came to about five thousand." The recording of results is first and foremost based on reports from the partner fellowship groups as one result of the partner group approach is that many are led to faith in Christ. CCT has introduced spiritual accountability and statistics are available also with respect to the number of groups that meet for Bible study, the number of participants and the number of people who profess faith in Christ. In 2010 there were 4,538 weekly Bible study groups spread throughout the country. Twenty-six churches were formed, initially meeting in the offices of CCT. The number of Muslim partners had reached 2,654. During 2010 some 1,090 street dwellers were fed; 1,290 scholarships were given to street dwellers for vocational training and forty street children were given education and housing assistance. About 444 weekly fellowship group meetings were conducted by community servants, themselves supervised by CCT project assistants. The same year there were 3,000 community servant leaders undergoing discipleship training with a view to deepening their faith.[16] By the end of 2009, 45,221 people were registered as having received Christ as Lord and Saviour and had been followed up through discipleship programs.[17] About 7 percent of the participants withdrew from the program in 2010. Withdrawing from the discipleship program does not have implications for their loans or other aspects of their status as CCT partners.

The next step for people who come to faith in Christ is to move them into discipleship training groups that are designed to equip them for life as Christians and later to assume responsibility for their own partner groups. A separate program is developed for disciple makers/group leaders based on *Practical Discipleship*, a leader's guide which is introduced with the key sentence: "Discipleship is not mere imparting of head knowledge, it is life transference . . . you should interact with the people you mentor, while all of you are being transformed by the Lord Jesus."[18] At that stage an individual may become a full partner in the Saving and Credit Cooperative which makes them participants and co-owners of the Cooperative.

Family transformation plays a key part in the CCT programs as the family constitutes a key unit in the fabric of a society. With a view to imparting knowledge of biblical teaching on the family a separate discipleship program has been developed for married couples. The teaching is viewed as an

---

16. CCT, *Serving like Jesus*, 62–65.
17. Callanta, *A Transformational Strategy*, 9.
18. Bertram Lim, *Practical Discipleship: Leader's Guide* (Manila: OMF, 1997), 5.

important vehicle for implementing the Great Commission: "Go and make disciples . . ." (Matt 28:19). The program addresses family issues, relationships, children, conflict handling, and so on, and thus new Christians are not left to grope around for themselves.[19]

As CCT employs microfinance not merely as a means to improve people's lives economically but also as a platform for transforming the individual and in turn families and communities, it employed an external evaluation agency, the Institute for Studies in Asian Church and Culture (ISACC), to study the effects of the programs. It was a qualitative survey based on interviews of 309 community partners and group discussions covering CCT activities in all of the Philippines. The main conclusion of the evaluation was positive: "The CCT offers a model for contextual development that other development practitioners in the Philippines may well learn from"; but it stresses at the same time that the CCT emphasis on the spiritual dimension "is not so much a matter of strategy as it is of identity."[20] The ISACC study also found that empowerment of women was evident in the testimonies of women, and that in general the CCT partners had experienced a lift that goes beyond economics.[21]

Economic and social transformation programs receive the approval of everybody, from individual sponsors to bilaterals and the UN/World Bank system. But a key component in spiritual transformation which is normally resisted by many donors, including bilateral and multilateral agencies, is to also extend to people an opportunity to know Christ. It is basic to the thinking in CCT that this can only happen if spiritual transformation constitutes a part of a social transformation program, a key component of which is the sharing of the gospel.[22]

On the basis of the recorded results of the operations of CCT it may be concluded that CCT is able to deliver on the third bottom line for Christian integral mission in the area of microfinance, that of ensuring that social action and proclamation are brought together along a timescale.

---

19. Bertram Lim, *Practical Discipleship for Married Couples* (Manila: OMF, 1997), 5.

20. Sylvia Palugod, Ruby Lavarias and Dolores Baltazar, *Joy in the Morning* (Queson City: Institute for Studies in Asian Church and Culture, 2000), 6.

21. Ibid., 6.

22. Callanta, *A Transformational Strategy*, 4.

4.1.7 The Handling of Mission Drift

It is right to ask how CCT has succeeded in handling the drivers of mission drift discussed in chapter 3. It tends not to be easy to detect mission drift. Microfinance organizations owned by Christians will always have some Christian leaders and employees. There will also be printed material aimed at different groups, such as sponsors, employing a Christian vocabulary which may be ambiguous in relation to Christian integral mission objectives.

CCT has been a fast-growth organization that could easily experience core value dilution if non-Christian professional staff who did not share the key values of the organization were recruited, and if they paid attention to the demands from sponsors to tone down evangelism, not only in mission statements but also in practice. Pressures on profit and the need for sustainability would make it just so much easier and tempting to yield to such demands. Also, it should not be forgotten that microfinance in the Philippines can be a very profitable operation if it is done in a certain way. Many organizations are susceptible to such attractions, as high income generation for the company at the same time strengthens career and salary prospects for the employees. All these factors could easily have led CCT into a situation of serious mission drift in relation to integral mission objectives.

How did CCT tackle this?

- *Top management support for spiritual transformation work.* One key feature of the holistic program is that it has top management support. In 2008 the board of CCT decided to lower the growth targets for the microfinance operation in order to avoid the situation where growth would be at the expense of quality in spiritual transformation and depth in relationships.
- *Resignation from the Opportunity International network* as CCT did not like what it felt was a primary emphasis on financials.
- *Creation of synergies in its operations.* In order to underpin the poverty focus, CCT tried to get synergies in the microfinance operations with other parts of the community services, primarily the health and education service units. For example, at the Training and Development institute of CCT in 2009, basic training in essential skills was given to 302 micro-entrepreneurs, basic business management training was given to 27 partners, and

modified bookkeeping and simplified accountancy training was given to 47 participants.[23]

- *Resistance of external pressures.* CCT resisted pressures from bilateral sponsors that advised them to drop Bible studies as they considered them economically non-productive, or to drop some formulations in the vision statement that include the proclamation of the gospel, in order to obtain funding. According to CCT management, the UN also wanted CCT to drop references to Christianity.

- *Staff embrace of key CCT values.* The decision to employ only professing evangelical Christians in CCT microfinance operations was of critical importance in their effort to avoid mission drift at the level of spiritual transformation. When the rapid growth in outreach in 2008 demanded a steep increase in the number of employees, the management put brakes on the pace of growth rather than recruit non-Christian staff. At the beginning of the work of CCT there were no such limitations for professional staff working in technical areas, such as development specialists. The management of CCT indicated that this did not work satisfactorily and they decided at a relatively early stage, in the mid-1990s, to embrace a personnel policy that ensured that all employees shared the value base of the organization.

- *A clarity of objectives* that has proven essential for success in spiritual transformation work. CCT management developed clear objectives in their operations in order to steer off mission drift. There is a conviction in CCT that microfinance is important because it leads to self-enrichment. At the same time there is an awareness that if economic enrichment is the main focus, a strategy involving spiritual transformation cannot be successful. Economic and social transformation is a technical operation, whereas spiritual transformation raises different demands upon the organization. Hence, if spiritual transformation is considered on a level with economic and social advance, this has to impact management policies, personnel policies, funding, fellowship studies, discipleship training, retreats, and so on.

---

23. CCT, *Serving Like Jesus*, 65.

- *A clear funding strategy.* CCT reported to me during the field work that the organization has been under pressure from external agencies, bilateral government agencies and multilateral international agencies to delete parts of the vision statement relating to introducing Christ in order to make it more politically correct, a requirement from the agencies if they are to extend funding to CCT. When such demands from external agencies are not met, the proposals to extend the much-needed funding are withdrawn. CCT has as a rule rejected such demands. Instead CCT has turned to financing sources which are favourable to the objectives of CCT, although it has meant slower growth. The most important funding source has become Christian business people in the Philippines who now have key positions on the board of the institution. But international Christian groups that sympathized with the explicit mission aim of CCT have also participated in the funding of the institution – for example, the Maranatha Trust of Australia.

The real strength of CCT is thus that overall mission objectives, strategies and operational plans are interlinked within the Transformational Development Framework (TDF) and that the whole development matrix of spiritual transformation is anchored in a unanimous conviction of direction among the top management and at board level.

4.2 Thailand and "Step Ahead"

4.2.1 Microfinance in Thailand

Thailand is a country with a population of close to 70 million people. It is estimated that 8.5 percent (5.5 million) of the population lived below the poverty line in 2007, earning less than Thai baht (THB) 1,433 per month. This is 14 percent of the country's gross national product per capita of THB 10,043 per month (using the UN benchmark of USD 1.25 per day). However, it is also estimated that 18 percent of the population (12 million) are "urban poor."[24]

---

24. *Microfinance Industry Report: Thailand* (South Brisbane, Queensland: Foundation for Development Cooperation, 2010), 6; available at Banking with the Poor Network, http://www.bwtp.org/files/Resources/Industry_Assesment/BWTP%20Network%20Thailand%20Microfinance%20Industry%20Report%20(English).pdf.

Although the Thai microfinance industry has been developed over a long time with a major concentration in rural areas, in comparison with the banks it has a relatively small role in lending in Thailand.[25] One important reason for this may be that in 2002 the Thai government expanded the services of two major state-owned banks to include loan services to small clients in both rural and urban areas. The Bank of Agriculture and Agricultural Cooperation (BAAC) and the Government Savings Bank today finance small-scale operations. The BAAC has the highest number of clients of all Thai financial institutions, and in excess of 93 percent of the farmers in the country have a loan account with BAAC. Therefore specialized MFOs do not have the same strong role in the market for small loans in urban and rural areas of Thailand as in the Philippines, where state banks have not been given this mandate. As there are fewer microfinance operators the competition in the main Thai cities might seem less fierce than in urban centres of some other Asian countries. However, the financial services to the poor in urban markets in Thailand are still dominated by the moneylenders.

The regulations of the NGO microfinance activities in Thailand lag behind those in the Philippines. It was a signal to the Thai government to take another look at the regulatory framework for the microfinance industry when one of the largest MFOs in Thailand, the Common Interest Foundation (CFI), closed its doors in July 2010. The main reason given by the investors behind CFI for this move was that the legal, fiscal and political frameworks were not satisfactory.[26]

4.2.2 Step Ahead (SA)

In contrast with CCT, SA has a small Christian microfinance organization operating within the framework of the integrated community program of the Step Ahead Foundation. SA is a community economic development foundation that partners with the poor with a view to helping them experience comprehensive and sustainable holistic transformation in their lives and in the lives of their families. When SA started in 2002 it was a micro-enterprise development program (MED); the foundation has since diversified its operations. The MED operations are in the largest slum in Bangkok, the

---

25. Ibid.

26. Microfinance Thailand, http://www.microfinancethailand.com/; accessed 10 November 2010.

Klong Toey area, and are operated in response to a great demand from the poor for credit on reasonable terms. The foundation is registered with the Thai government as a non-profit humanitarian organization. The mission statement of SA is "to amalgamate microfinance, mentoring, community economic development, and capacity building into an integrated service that powerfully displays the love of God while actively developing and empowering the poor, vulnerable and the marginalized."[27]

In addition to the microfinance the integral mission activities of SA also include four child development centres in Khao Lak, southern Thailand, to help women and children at risk, orphan programs, a program to combat human trafficking (Pattaya) and a program that attends to communities at risk of human exploitation in the poor northeast of Thailand. The Khao Lak office has twenty-five full-time Thai staff and foreign volunteers leverage the staff to increase program impact. The child development centres started in 2010 with 135 children attending them. They serve over 600 members of the community with training workshops to help the teachers and families develop their personal capacities in a number of areas, such as nutrition, family finances and family planning. The community economic development program provides training in gardening and raising livestock through a seed project.

SA has a special focus on women and children at risk. With the help of SA staff projects have been started to help women at risk of entering the sex trade. The projects in Pattaya and the northeast employ women at risk to produce leather purses and woven leather products to increase their economic opportunities. In addition there is a Keeping Families Together program that assists families in keeping their children rather than sending them to an orphanage due to poverty conditions and lack of resources. SA also partners with industry, UNESCO, Thai church leaders and the Thai government with a view to helping families with young girls understand the risk of sending their daughters to work in the big cities and to helping the young people stay in school.

---

27. Step Ahead Integrated Community Development Foundation, *Vision, Mission, Values: Annual Report 2009–2010* (Bangkok: Step Ahead, 2010), 3.

4.2.3 The Operational Framework of SA and Financial Sustainability

The operational model of SA is different from that of CCT. SA practises individual lending without a group collateral, but rather with an individual guarantee which should come from another individual who has a job. Initially SA attempted to implement the widespread microfinance model of individual lending with group solidarity guarantees, but the experience of SA was that this did not work satisfactorily in the poor urban setting of Bangkok. Unlike in Manila, in the cultural context of urban Bangkok it turned out that group members were not willing to pay up if other members in the group defaulted. In 2010 there were 1,200 clients partnering with SA. They were serviced by a small staff of one chief operations officer and four credit officers and an accountant, all Christian Thai nationals. The normal loan size is THB 3,000 (approximately USD 100). SA also charges a 15 percent membership fee which is collected up front. Thus all clients are also SA members, and the words "member" and "client" are synonyms. The loans have a five-month repayment period and collections are made on a weekly basis. The total volume of client loans is USD 100,000. The capital base is approximately 1 million THB, the equivalent of USD 33,000.

The SA mission activities in Bangkok are integrated community services to serve the poor and afflicted. Also, the accounts of the activities are integrated. Thus SA does not have separate accounts for the microfinance activities. The financial result for the overall activities including donations shows that the income stream can finance the costs of the overall mission operations. However, in order to arrive at an estimate of the degree of financial sustainability for the microfinance operations, I undertook a special study in cooperation with the director of the Step Ahead Foundation. In the analysis carried out the expenses and revenues that related to microfinance were identified: interest income, salaries of microfinance employees, the share of microfinance of the costs of rent, maintenance, and so on. The analysis indicated that the microfinance operations of SA are not self-financing. On an annual basis the microfinance operations need to cover about 40 percent of their overall expenses through donor support.

SA informed me that some expert observers from the Christian microfinance community had recommended that SA terminate their microfinance operations. The reasons given were that they had not grown much and did not appear financially sustainable after eight years of operations, and that most likely they were not going to be self-financing for some time to come. SA management rejected this view. The motivation for SA to embrace microfinance as a platform for their integral mission activities is that microfinance in their view is a unique way of reaching out to poor people and their families with the gospel. It seems reasonable to argue that in terms of integral mission there is no difference in principle between using donor funds to combat human trafficking and child abuse, and injecting donor funds into microfinance for poverty eradication. It is all considered integral mission, alleviating misery and poverty coupled with the sharing of the gospel with the target group in order to give people the opportunity to experience spiritual transformation.

This approach to the use of microfinance throws a different light on Christian microfinance activities. The idea that Christian microfinance should in all circumstances be financially viable may not be valid within an integral mission framework. The SA management informed me during the site visit that microfinance for them is important both with respect to helping the poor break out of the poverty trap and to providing a platform for evangelism.

It seems likely that the employment of an integrated mission platform using microfinance as a vehicle in a country with a narrow Christian recruitment base will often not be self-sustaining. Therefore the right question for a Christian mission to ask before opting for the use of microfinance as a vehicle for integral mission in a country with a small Christian minority that constitutes a limited recruitment base for microfinance may not be whether microfinance will be financially viable or not. Rather it may be right to ask whether the net cost of running the microfinance operations – and which has to be financed by donor funds – can be justified by the opportunities it gives for assisting the poor and sharing the gospel. It is legitimate to argue that the use of microfinance in integral Christian mission is not dependent on whether it is financially sustainable or not, but on whether it is an effective vehicle for Christian mission in its own right. It is quite possible to have a Christian-owned MFO in Thailand that is self-sustaining by high-volume operations ensured by the employment of local non-Christian Thais. However, it might be questioned whether such a strategy would give the MFO a Christian integral mission profile.

It may thus be concluded that the microfinance operations of SA are not financially sustainable. However, in the light of the use SA makes of microfinance it may be questioned whether the first bottom line – that microfinance should be financially viable – should be accepted as a requirement for measuring success in a country with a small Christian minority. Expected financial viability has not been crucial for SA's choice of microfinance as a vehicle for integral mission. Rather the choice was motivated by the potential of microfinance to help poor people and at the same time constitute a platform for evangelism.

4.2.4 Target Groups, Poverty Eradication and Results

The SA Microfinance Enterprises Development (MED) in the Klong Toey slum area in Bangkok is targeting primarily poor women to assist them to build their businesses and provide for their families. The target group belongs to the large section of Thai society which is termed the urban poor. The average income of the target group is estimated to be below the poverty line for city dwellers in Thailand of THB 1,433 per month. Prior to SA MED operations, when in need of credit, members of the local community served by SA had to access the local moneylenders who charge a minimum of 20 percent interest per month.[28] The high interest rates charged by the moneylenders reduce the probability that the micro-businesses will grow and become sustainable. Loans with such high interest rates are difficult to service and the result is often a high indebtedness which curtails the business prospects of micro-enterprises of poor people. Through the microfinance program in 2010, 1,200 clients were actively served.

SA partners actively with the members of the MED, and besides giving them access to reasonably priced finance they also provide business training, mentoring and counselling, and personal development courses. All the services are provided by SA staff members who have developed a long and stable working relationship with the members in the course of their business. Due to the synergies that have been achieved between the different ministries in SA it is likely that SA has a beneficial impact, in addition to the 1,200 microfinance clients in 2010, on the lives of 5,000 people in the Klong Toey area. It is thus estimated that in excess of 6,000 people were served through the microfinance integral mission program in the Klong Toey slum. This estimate is based on the number of people who participate in the various programs.

Taking into account the location of the SA operations and the general living standard of people living in the slums of Klong Toey, and observations

---

28. Sriduda Supsin, "Microfinance," in *Annual Report 2009–2010 Step Ahead Integrated Community Development* (Bangkok: Step Ahead, 2010), 6.

of the clients and their families during the field visits, it may be concluded that SA has a clear poverty eradication focus. It may also be concluded that SA is able to deliver quite successfully on the second bottom line of Christian microfinance, that of delivering a socially beneficial service to the poor.

4.2.5 Holistic Mission and Spiritual Transformation

The objective and the operational model of SA microfinance activities are identical to those of CCT: to use microfinance for poverty eradication and to let this social action program serve as a platform for evangelism, in this case specifically stated as "helping Thais to reach their destiny in Christ."[29] In one sense it may be right to say that SA and CCT have the same "DNA imprint," as SA management at an early stage, in 2002, received training for integral mission in microfinance in CCT. SA contextualized this concept of integral mission to the Buddhist culture of Thailand and the result is an SA operation that in many ways is distinctly different from that of CCT.

There are a number of synergies between the microfinance operations and the various social services which are developed by the organization for their clients and the community surrounding the microfinance operations. SA offers English and computer skills training to youth in the Klong Toey community which will improve their chances of obtaining jobs at a later stage in their lives. The foundation also runs a Kids' Club which has a weekly program that gives children in the community the opportunity to have safe fun. Both programs are aimed at injecting hope into the community as they are mentored by SA staff who want to be positive influences in their lives.

In addition SA facilitates for the women members a twice-yearly breast cancer screening service. In 2010 more than 300 clients received a free women's health check from Queen Sirikit Center for Breast Cancer. SA registered that their staff had spent more than 13,500 hours of mentoring, coaching, counselling and capacity building.[30]

The cultural challenge for evangelism is real. In the Buddhist cultural context of Thailand the model for evangelism is necessarily different from that of CCT. Arranging meetings with presentations or study groups do not function as well in the slums of Bangkok as in the Philippines. There is a

---

29. Step Ahead, http://www.ywamthai.org/bangkok/stepahead.htm; accessed 10 November 2010.

30. Step Ahead, *Vision, Mission, Values*, 6.

considerable time span between the time of first contact with a person and the time when he or she can understand the fundamentals of the Christian faith. Hence the microfinance programs are run with the anticipation that over time, during the personal contact between SA staff and the members and their families, there will also be opportunities for sharing the Christian faith. SA maintains that in order to communicate the gospel effectively to individuals brought up with Buddhist karma thinking and the pantheistic thought models of Buddhism a lengthy time of pre-evangelism is required – a period during which the Christian concept of God and the context of salvation may slowly be understood.

The evangelism part of SA integral mission is adapted to the operational model of the organization. Because SA does not employ the group solidarity model in its lending, tight-knit client groups cannot be used as a basis for Bible studies and evangelism. The major emphasis is shifted to personal evangelism. The credit officers are in weekly contact with each client. The clients are from a Buddhist background and as it takes a long time to communicate the substance of Christianity to them the SA approach is to build friendships through microfinance contacts. The work is done in anticipation of opportunities to share the gospel with clients and their families. In addition, members of the microfinance work of SA are invited to come to monthly SA member gatherings at which there is Bible study led by SA staff prior to discussions on financial matters. The broadest point of contact between SA and the members is therefore the personal involvement of the credit officers in the lives of the clients. The relatively low number of clients for which each member of staff is responsible (approximately two hundred) gives room for more personal follow-up of clients in SA than is normal in microfinance operations.

There is, however, no exact registry developed for the effects of evangelism, although some strong anecdotal evidence was presented to me during the field work which suggested that at times the response to the proclamation of the gospel has been profoundly felt. It should be kept in mind that spiritual transformation processes in a Thai culture are protracted and SA continues the integral mission efforts in the anticipation that the communication of the gospel will give specific results along a fairly long timescale. The role of the church is also important in SA. The local churches are partnering in the follow-up of individuals, and the pastor of the nearest small local church is actively involved in SA activities. The churches, however, are not involved at the level of financial transactions with individuals in the ongoing microfinance activities.

On the basis of the observed operations of SA it may be concluded that SA is able to deliver on the third bottom line for Christian integral mission, that of ensuring that social action and proclamation are brought together along a timescale.

4.2.6 The Handling of Mission Drift

Whereas CCT operates in a country that is predominantly Catholic, SA operates in an environment that is approximately 98 percent Buddhist and there is only a relatively small Christian church in the country. There is ample scope for growth in a microfinance operation in Bangkok. However, the scarcity of available Christian staff candidates impacts severely the possibilities of SA to cope with high growth while at the same time maintaining microfinance as a platform for integral mission. In spite of that SA has maintained a strong spiritual transformation objective since its inception and resisted mission drift in relation to integral mission objectives. How has SA tackled this?

- *Through organizational commitment.* The organization remains highly committed to maintaining the poverty eradication program as a platform for Christian mission. In order to maintain and develop SA as a vehicle for integral mission the management of SA have not given priority to volume growth.
- *A staff that embraces the Christian value base of SA.* In a predominantly Buddhist country with few Christians an important obstacle to growth is the shortage of Christian believers who also have the necessary skills for working with microfinance. SA rejected at an early stage the option to hire non-Christians for its operations in the awareness that accepting such a personnel policy would weaken its efforts to maintain a vibrant Christian witness in relation to the Buddhist client base. A potential source of recruitment (mentioned by SA) is people who have become Christians as a result of the work of SA or other missions and churches in the country. Without a pool of Christian workers to draw from, SA has chosen a slow-growth strategy, thereby staying committed to its vision to use microfinance as a platform for integral mission.

- *Restrictive funds mobilization.* SA has not wanted to increase significantly the inflow of funds for microfinance so as not to place unnecessary pressure on the organization to expand. Fundraising is closely linked to the ability to absorb increased funding through growth in outreach. However, the institution requires a steady inflow of donor capital to be sustainable in the long run, and this coupled with intensified efforts to identify Thai national Christians interested in working among the poor may enable SA to achieve more growth in the future without compromising its vision to be a vehicle for integral Christian mission in Thailand.

4.3 Summary of Case Studies

The main difference between the operations of CCT and SA and those of other Christian microfinance organizations encountered in the course of the field study is at the level of vision and context. Both CCT and SA considered their microfinance organization as a vehicle for evangelism and this vision was decisive in the design of their strategies. The activities of their microfinance operations consist of two legs: product delivery and poverty alleviation activities, and evangelism. CCT has clearly been the most successful of the two in terms of growth based on an integral mission strategy. The operations of SA, although on a much smaller scale, show that it is possible to maintain microfinance as an instrument for spiritual transformation activities even in a culture which limits the possibilities for accessing the most critical input factor for integral mission: a pool from which to recruit employees who share the core values of the organization. But the two case studies also indicate that a microfinance operation that is run on the integral mission principles of CCT and SA as described above can grow and expand only to the extent that it is able to employ Christian employees who both share the core values of the organization and have the right qualifications for microfinance. In cultures with relatively small Christian communities like Thailand it may be expected that the integral mission model of CCT/SA will have a limited growth potential. The SA operation is a clear indication of that.

The two organizations are also distinctly different in the area of financial sustainability. The microfinance operations of SA are not financially sustainable while the CCT operations are highly financially sustainable. However, in the light of the use SA makes of microfinance it may be questioned whether the first bottom line – that microfinance must be financially viable – should be accepted as a requirement for measuring success in a country with a small Christian minority. Expected financial viability has not been crucial for SA's choice of microfinance as a vehicle for integral mission. Rather the choice was motivated by the potential of microfinance to help poor people and at the same time constitute a platform for evangelism. Therefore, a Christian mission organization considering whether to use microfinance as a vehicle for integral mission in a country with a small Christian minority that constitutes a limited recruitment base for microfinance may not necessarily give a decisive importance to the potential financial viability of the microfinance. The right question to ask may rather be whether the cost of supporting the microfinance operations with donor funds can be justified by the opportunities it gives for assisting the poor and sharing the gospel.

The findings indicate that CCT and SA have spiritual transformation strategies for their microfinance operations which are distinctly driven by a Christian integral mission model. However, the study also shows that spiritual transformation processes in a Thai culture are much more protracted than those in a predominantly Catholic Philippine culture. SA maintains the integral mission efforts in the anticipation that the communication of the gospel will give specific results along a longer timescale than in the Philippines.

5

Summary and Conclusions

This study has explored the effects of "mission drift" in the context of the paradigm shift in the understanding of Christian mission as it has evolved through the Lausanne process. In microfinance the concept of "mission drift" is used to describe how MFOs often gradually drift away from serving the poor in order to maintain financial sustainability. This study employs an expanded use of "mission drift" to describe the extent to which microfinance activities run by Christian mission organizations may for various reasons also drift away from the integral mission objective of sharing the gospel of Christ and leading poor people into a process of spiritual transformation.

Christian MFOs are part of a major microfinance industry, and as they draw on both personnel and financial resources in the church at large it is important that a clearer picture of the extent of tendencies toward "mission drift" in microfinance activities of Christian mission is established. Only thus may shortcomings be rectified and deviations from a biblical mission platform be removed.

This thesis has explored the evolution of the integral mission concept in the context of the Lausanne movement. The study indicates that there is a broad consensus in the evangelical community that integral mission constitutes the basis for biblically based Christian mission efforts, to proclaim the gospel of Christ in word and to embody it in social action with a view to improving the total life situation of the poor and oppressed. Without an element of verbal proclamation of the gospel in the context of social action the latter may have beneficial social effects, but this study indicates that it is not Christian mission as defined in the course of the Lausanne process. The study in chapter 2 also highlighted the need for more clarity with respect both to the integral mission concept itself and to how to implement it. It is a paradox that an indirect cause of mission drift may be the paradigm shift in Christian mission thinking itself. The lack of clarity is exemplified by the continuous "priority of evangelism" debate and the issue of what is the right balance between social action and evangelism.

I have discussed various attempts at clarifying the balance, and I propose the use of the term "anticipation" of evangelism instead of "primacy" or "ultimacy." In integral mission theology, the twin activities – social action and evangelism – should go together, although not always in real time. "Anticipation" of evangelism might better reflect the view that social action may create a bridge for evangelism, and it might also take care of the concern of many that evangelism should never be left undone. Finally, "anticipation" contains a stronger reference to the need for a time and planning element in Christian integral mission.

The present lack of clarity as to what the integral mission concept entails at the implementation stage may be an important explanatory factor for why proclamation of the gospel may gradually be weakened. This happens particularly in those areas of Christian social action where successful growth requires a personnel policy that ensures the recruitment of high numbers of new employees with special qualifications. Christian microfinance is such an area. One reason for this is that it may be difficult to find a sufficient number of interested, qualified Christian candidates to fill the vacant positions in a fast-growing MFO. Thus, even when the theology of mission of an NGO or a church is soundly based on an integral mission concept, over time the strength of proclamation may slowly be impaired because of professional and cultural pressures.

In chapter 3, the biblical understanding of the poor and poverty was viewed in relation to a discussion of how to identify and define the appropriate target group for the delivery of Christian microfinance services. It was argued that the biblical understanding of poverty, which includes spiritual poverty, should have far-reaching consequences for the strategy of Christian MFOs. In particular it impacts the understanding of how to design poverty abatement strategies in Christian microfinance organizations that want to reflect integral mission concerns: that the operations should be multifaceted and holistic, integrating abatement of economic poverty with spiritual transformation. The chapter also indicated that Christian microfinance organizations are confronted with several mission drift drivers in relation to Christian integral mission objectives. As Christian MFOs are under much pressure to ensure long-term financial sustainability, the key drivers for mission drift tend to be high-volume growth, the recruitment of non-Christian personnel who cannot take active part in holistic mission activities, lack of clarity and understanding of the integral mission concept, cultural pressures and the need to ensure external funding from agencies that make funding conditional upon non-proclamation of the gospel.

The study indicated that most of the lending of Christian MFOs targets poor clients. However, even though the available evidence indicates that microfinance tends not to have income effects of such magnitude that most poor borrowers break out of the poverty trap, the lending nevertheless tends to have the effect of "consumption smoothing," which in itself is beneficial and important for poor households in that it reduces their vulnerability. The study has shown that there is a risk of mission drift in relation to the objective to deliver a social good to the poor, but that such risks may be fairly easily addressed.

On the other hand, the risk of mission drift in Christian MFOs tends to be more serious in relation to the proclamation part of Christian integral mission than in relation to the delivery of a social good to the poor. Although mission drift in relation to spiritual transformation is difficult to measure, the increased commercialization of microfinance makes it difficult for Christian MFOs to cope with the extra costs and the demand on human resources that a holistic and spiritual transformation strategy entails. There are indications that this in turn may result in mission drift in relation to holistic objectives.

As I in the course of the study became more aware of the serious pressures on Christian microfinance toward mission drift in relation to the proclamation part of integral mission, this led me to ask whether Christian microfinance has the potential to be a viable platform for integral mission. With this question in mind I decided to conduct a field study in the Philippines and in Thailand. The main part of the study referred to in chapter 4 was in the Philippines, which has a more developed microfinance industry than Thailand. The field study shows that a microfinance operation does not become integral mission simply because it is owned by a Christian organization, but because the organization itself is aware of the mechanisms that produce mission drift and takes the necessary steps to counteract them. The field research in the Philippines and Thailand shows that the risks of mission drift are real, but also that they may be overcome by Christian MFOs who are aware of their existence. The two institutions highlighted in this study, the Centre for Community Transformation in the Philippines and Step Ahead in Thailand, illustrate that delivering a social good to the poor is not incompatible with using microfinance as a platform for evangelism. However, the study showed differences with respect to financial sustainability, as the microfinance operations of SA are not financially sustainable while the CCT operations are highly financially sustainable. The study shows that there are good reasons to question whether the first bottom line – that microfinance should be financially viable – should be accepted as a requirement for measuring success in a country with a small Christian minority. It was the potential of microfinance to help poor people, and at the same time constitute a platform for evangelism, that motivated SA's choice of microfinance as a vehicle for mission, not its expected financial viability.

The field study suggests that Christian MFOs that have pursued growth without paying attention to the requirements of integral mission tend to suffer mission drift in relation to the proclamation part of an integral mission objective. Without a personnel policy that ensures a broad-based Christian staff in the organization it is necessarily difficult to pursue integral mission that employs microfinance as a platform or bridge for evangelism. The same goes for the choice of funding strategy for a Christian MFO. If it has yielded to pressures from governmental or private financing sources to soften its mission statement by deleting its core mission intent to proclaim the gospel, this will necessarily impact the way the organization will work. With Christian personnel in all areas of the institution and funding sponsors that do not object to evangelism, the MFO will be free to develop strategies to carry out its mission, both in the poverty abatement work among the poor and in spiritual transformation strategies involving both the employees and the clients.

Some areas have been outside the scope of this thesis but are clearly in need of more research. First, it would improve our understanding of the operations of Christian MFOs if the extent of mission drift in a larger population of Christian MFOs could be established. Such a study would require a more representative sample of Christian MFOs in the world. Second, it would be useful to know more of how Christian MFOs that experience serious mission drift may adjust their operations. For such institutions it would be important to clarify whether or not it is feasible in organizational terms to make partial adjustment to the operations so that they may gradually move back in line with integral mission objectives. It would also be useful to explore further how microfinance could be run by a Christian organization in countries with a limited supply of potential Christian employees (e.g. Thailand) and yet be able to achieve significant growth and outreach combined with success in relation to integral mission objectives in the area of evangelism.

It may very well be that some institutions have seen the risks for mission drift but have ignored them because taking them into account might have come at a price – that is, lower growth and lower income. Thus the main focus of many Christian MFOs has been on improving the financial parameters to sharpen productivity and improve competitiveness, profitability and long-term funding for high growth. The high profitability of MFOs that are professionally run may easily tempt Christian organizations to operate merely as microfinance organizations and not as integral missions. Such Christian MFOs may be satisfied with the service which is rendered to the poor by including them in the financial system. That is a valuable service, but without evangelism it is not integral mission as defined by the evangelical world during the course of the Lausanne process.

Bibliography

African Development Bank Group. "Microfinance Operations Have Difficulty Reaching the Very Poor." 1 December 2010, accessed 6 May 2011, http://www.afdb.org/en/news-and-events/article/microfinance-operations-have-difficulty-reaching-the-very-poor-7548/.

Alliance of Philippine Partners in Enterprise Development Incorporated (APPEND). *Household Chores*. Manila: Timotheos Publishing, 2008.

Anglican Communion. Accessed 11 November 2010, http://www.anglicancommunion.org/ministry/mission/fivemarks.cfm.

Banerjee, Abhijit, Esther Duflo, Rachel Glennerster and Cynthia Kinnan. "Measuring the Impact of Microfinance in Hyderabad, India." The Abdul Latif Jameel Poverty Action Lab. Accessed 11 November 2010, http://www.povertyactionlab.org/.

Bebbington, David W. *Evangelicalism in Modern Britain: A History from the 1730s to the 1980s*. London: Routledge, 1989.

Bergem, Anders. *Kristen Tro og profesjonell omsorg*. Translated from Norwegian: Christian Faith and Professional Care. Oslo: Luther forlag, 1998.

Billy Graham Center Archives. "The Wheaton Declaration." Accessed 10 November 2010, http://www.wheaton.edu/bgc/archives/docs/wd66/b08.html.

Blomberg, Craig L. *Neither Poverty Nor Riches: A Biblical Theology of Possessions*. Downers Grove: Inter-Varsity Press, 1999.

Bosch, David J. *Transforming Mission: Paradigm Shifts in Theology of Mission*. New York: Orbis, 2008.

Brierley, Peter. "Evangelicals in the World of the 21st Century." In *2004 Forum on World Evangelization Program*. Lausanne: LCWE, 2004.

Bruce F. F. *Paul: Apostle of the Free Spirit*. Carlisle: Paternoster, 1995.

———. *The Spreading Flame*. Exeter: Paternoster, 1982.

Bussau, David, and Russell Mask. *Christian Microenterprise Development: An Introduction*. Oxford: Regnum Books, 2003.

BWTP Network, "The Microfinance Report: Thailand." Accessed 2 October 2010, http://www.bwtp.org/news/?p=285.

Callanta, Ruth S. *A Transformational Strategy*. Manila: CCT, 2009.

CCT. *Serving Like Jesus: Yearbook 2009*. Manila: CCT Group of
   Ministries, 2010.

CCT Group of Ministries. "Organizational Primer." Undated, unpublished
   in-house document, Manila.

Centre for Research Development & Technology Transfer. "Understanding
   Beneficiaries Livelihood of Norwegian Mission Alliance's Micro Finance
   Program in the Tien Giang Province, Mekong Delta Vietnam." Bin
   Duong University, Binh Duong, December 2006.

Chambers, Robert. *Rural Development: Putting the Last First*. London:
   Longman, 1983.

Chester, Tim. *Good News to the Poor*. Nottingham: IVP, 2004.

Copestake, James, Martin Greely, Susan Johnson, Naila Kabeer and Anton
   Simanowitz. *Money with a Mission: Microfinance and Poverty Reduction*.
   Bourton-on-Dunsmore: ITDG, 2005.

Danel, Carlos. "Are We drifting Yet?" CGAP. 25 October 2010, accessed
   4 November 2010, http://microfinance.cgap.org/2010/10/25/are-we-
   drifting-yet/.

Dichter, Thomas. "A Second Look at Microfinance: The Sequence of Growth
   and Credit in Economic History." Cato Institute, Washington DC
   Development Policy Briefing Paper, 15 February 2007.

———, and Malcolm Harper. *What's Wrong with Microfinance?* Rugby:
   Intermediate Technology Publications, 2007.

Dictionary.com. "Anticipation." Accessed 14 May 2010, http://dictionary.
   reference.com/browse/anticipation.

Dudley-Smith, Timothy. *John Stott: A Global Ministry*. Leicester: Inter-
   Varsity Press, 2001.

The Economist. "Economic Focus: A Partial Marvel." 16 July 2009, http://
   www.economist.com/node/14031284.

Eldred, Ken. *God Is at Work, Transforming People and Nations through
   Business*. Montrose: Manna Ventures, 1995.

Engel, James F., and William A. Dyrness. *Changing the Mind of Missions:
   Where Have We Gone Wrong?* Downers Grove: IVP, 2000.

Fee, G. D. *The First Epistle to the Corinthians*. NICNT. Grand Rapids:
   Eerdmans, 1987.

Fikkert, Brian. "Christian Microfinance: Which Way Now?" Paper
   prepared for the Association of Christian Economists 20th
   Anniversary Conference, 5–6 January 2003. Chalmers University.

Accessed 21 February 2010, www.chalmers.org/resources/documents/workingpaper205.pdf.

The Free Dictionary. Accessed 4 November 2010, http//:www.thefreedictionary.com/drift.

Friedman, John. *Empowerment: The Politics of Alternative Development.* Cambridge: Blackwell, 1992.

Giné, Xavier, Tomoko Harigaya, Dean Karlan et al. "Evaluating Microfinance Program Innovation with Randomized Control Trials: An Example from Group Versus Individual Lending." Yale University, March 2006, accessed 12 November 2010, http://karlan.yale.edu/p/ADB_TN16.pdf.

Gokhale, Ketaki. "A Global Surge in Tiny Loans Spurs Credit Bubble in a Slum." *Wall Street Journal*, 13 August 2009; at Allianz, accessed 30 August 2010, http://knowledge.allianz.com/en/globalissues/microfinance/microcredit/microfinance_debt_trap.html.

Gonzalez, Adrian. "Microfinance at a Glance – 2008. Updated on December 31, 2009." Microfinance Information Exchange (MIX). Accessed 4 May 2010, http://www.themix.org/sites/default/files/Microfinance%20at%20a%20Glance%202009-12-31.pdf.

Grant, Jamie A., and Dewi A. Hughes. *Transforming the World? The Gospel and Social Responsibility.* Nottingham: Inter-Varsity Press, 2009.

Gray, Sherman W. *The Least of My Brothers: Matthew 25.31–46: A History of Interpretation.* Atlanta: Scholars Press, 1989.

Greeley, Martin. "Sustainable Poverty Outreach." In James Copestake, Martin Greely, Susan Johnson, Naila Kabeer and Anton Simanowitz, *Money with a Mission: Microfinance and Poverty Reduction*, 21–45. Bourton-on-Dunsmore: ITDG, 2005.

Green, Joel B. *The Theology of the Gospel of Luke.* New Testament Theology. Cambridge: Cambridge University Press, 1995.

Greer, Peter, and Phil Smith. *The Poor Will Be Glad: Joining the Revolution to Lift the World Out of Poverty.* Grand Rapids: Zondervan, 2009.

Harford, Tim. "The Battle for the Soul of Microfinance." *FT Magazine*, 6 December 2008, http://www.ft.com/cms/s/0/8080c698-c0d2-11dd-b0a8-000077b07658.html.

Heldt, Jean-Paul. "Revisiting the Whole Gospel: Towards a Biblical Model of Holistic Mission in the 21st Century." *Missiology* 32 (2004): 149–72.

HOPE International. Accessed 27 March 2010, http://www.hopeinternational.org/about-hope/.

Hulme, D., and P. Mosley. *Finance Against Poverty.* 2 vols. London: Routledge, 1996.

International Opportunity. Accessed 27 March 2010, http://www.opportunity.org/.

Jayakaran, Ravi. "Holistic Participatory Learning and Action: Seeing the Spiritual and Whose Reality Counts." In *Walking with the Poor: New Insights and Learnings from Development Practitioners*, edited by Bryant Myers, 80. Monrovia, CA: MARC, 1999.

Johnson, Susan, and Ben Rogaly. *Microfinance and Poverty Reduction.* Oxford: Oxfam and Action Aid, 1997.

Jongeneel, J. A. B. "Mission Theology in the Twentieth Century." In *Dictionary of Mission Theology: Evangelical Foundations*, edited by John Corrie, 237–44. Nottingham: Inter-Varsity Press, 2007.

Kirk, Andrew. *Mission Under Scrutiny: Considering Current Challenges.* London: Darton, Longman & Todd, 2006.

———. *What Is Mission? Theological Explorations.* Minneapolis: Fortress Press, 2000.

KMBI. Accessed 28 September 2010, http:www.kmbi.org.ph/index.php?option=com_content&view=article&id=98&Itemi.

Kunzemann, Thilo. "Is Micro-finance a Debt Trap?" Allianz. Accessed 14 March 2010, http://knowledge.allianz.com/en/globalissues/microfinance/microcredit/microfinance_debt_trap.html.

Ladd, George Eldon. "The Parable of the Sheep and the Goats in Recent Interpretation." In *New Dimensions in New Testament Study*, edited by Richard N. Longernecker and Merrill C. Tenney, 191. Grand Rapids: Zondervan, 1974.

Lausanne Movement. "Manila Manifesto." Accessed 6 May 2011, http://www.lausanne.org/content/manifesto/the-manila-manifesto.

Lausanne Occasional Paper (LOP) 21. "Evangelism and Social Responsibility: An Evangelical Commitment." Joint publication of the Lausanne Committee for World Evangelization (LCWE) and the World Evangelical Fellowship (WEF). Lausanne Movement. 1982, accessed 10 January 2010, http://www.lausanne.org/content/lop/lop-21.

Ledesma, Jesila M., and Ma. Chona O. David-Casis. *Mission First: SPM Advocacy in the Philippines.* Pasig City: Microfinance Council of the Philippines, 2010.

Lim, Bertram. *Practical Discipleship: Leader's Guide.* Manila: OMF, 1997.

———. *Practical Discipleship for Married Couples.* Manila: OMF, 1997.

McGrath, A. E. *Evangelism and the Future of Christianity.* London: Hodder & Stoughton, 1988.

Mersland, Roy. "The Governance of Non-Profit Micro Finance Institutions: Lessons from History." University of Agder, 6 October 2009, SpringerLink. Accessed 10 October 2010, www.Springerlink.com/index/256132t07065267x.pdf, 5.

———. "On the Impact of Religion in the Microfinance Industry: A Multidimensional Comparison of Catholic, Protestant, and Non-religious Microfinance Organizations." Unpublished working paper, University of Agder, Norway, 2010.

———, and Øystein Strøm. "Microfinance Mission Drift? Description and Explanation." *World Development* 38, no. 1 (2010): 28–36. Elserver. Accessed 4 November 2010, www.elserver.com/locate/worlddev.

Micah Network. "Micah Declaration on Integral Mission." Accessed 5 March 2010, http://www.micahnetwork.org/.

Microfinance Council of the Philippines. "2009 Annual Report." Manila, 2010.

Microfinance Thailand. Accessed 10 November 2010, http://www.microfinancethailand.com/.

Murdoch, Jonathan. "Does Microfinance Really Help the Poor? New Evidence from Flagship Programs in Bangladesh." Published paper, Harvard University, 1998.

Myers, Bryant L. *Walking with the Poor: Principles and Practices of Transformational Development.* New York: Orbis, 2008.

Neill, Stephen. *Creative Tension.* London: Edinburgh House Press, 1959.

Newman, Barclay M., Jr. *A Concise Greek–English Dictionary of the New Testament.* Stuttgart: Deutsche Bibelgesellschaft, 1993.

Nida, Eugene A., and Johannes P. Louw. *Greek–English Lexicon of the New Testament Based on Semantic Domains.* Vol. 1. New York: United Bible Societies, 1988–89.

OECD. "Poverty Line: Glossary of Statistical Terms." Accessed 4 May 2010, http://stats.oecd.org/glossary/detail.asp?ID=6337.

———. "When Money Is Tight: Poverty Dynamics in OECD Countries." OECD Employment Outlook. Accessed 4 May 2010, http://www.oecd.org/dataoecd/29/55/2079296.pdf, p. 41.

Opportunity International. Accessed 27 March 2010, www.opportunity.org/.

Packer, J. I. *"Fundamentalism" and the Word of God.* London: IVP, 1965.

Padilla, C. René. "Holistic Mission." In *Dictionary of Mission Theology: Evangelical Foundations*, edited by John Corrie, 157–62. Downers Grove: IVP, 2007.

———. *Misión integral: Ensayos sobre el Reino y la Iglesia*. Grand Rapids: Eerdmans, 1986.

———. *Mission Between the Times*. Grand Rapids: Eerdmans, 1985.

———, and Chris Sugden, eds. *How Evangelicals Endorsed Social Responsibility*. Bramcote: Grove, 1985.

Palugod, Sylvia, Ruby Lavarias and Dolores Baltazar. *Joy in the Morning*. Queson City: Institute for Studies in Asian Church and Culture, 2000.

Philippine Statistics Authority National Statistical Coordination Board (NSCB). Projection on the 2007 survey on population. NSCB. http://www.census.gov/ph.

Profin Foundation. "Study of Impact and Client Satisfaction with the Loan Services of Diaconia-Frif: An Independent Evaluation." Appraisal paper, La Paz, March 2009.

Provention Consortium. Accessed 5 November 2010, http://www.proventionconsortium.org/themes/default/pdfs/tools_for_mainstreaming_GN10.pdf.

Robinson, Howard. "Dualism." Stanford Encyclopedia of Philosophy. Rev. 3 November 2011, http://plato.stanford.edu/contents.html.

Rosenberg, Richard. "Does Microcredit Really Help Poor People?" CGAP. 5 October 2009, accessed 15 March 2010, http://www.cgap.org/blog/does-microcredit-really-help-poor-people.

Samuel, Vinay and Albrecht Hauser, eds. *Proclaiming Christ in Christ's Way: Studies in Integral Mission*. Eugene: Wipf & Stock, 1989.

Schaeffer F. *Trilogy: The God Who Is There; Escape from Reason; He Is There and He Is Not Silent*. Wheaton: Crossway, 1990.

Sharma, Dr Sudhirendar. "Are Microfinance Institutions Exploiting the Poor?" Infochange: Poverty. August 2006, accessed 10 April 2010, http://infochangeindia.org/20060802286/Poverty/Analysis/Are-micro-finance-institutions-exploiting-the-poor.html.

Sider, Ronald. With James Parker. "How Broad Is Salvation in Scripture?" In *In Word and Deed*, edited by Bruce Nicholls, 89–99. Carlisle: Paternoster, 1985.

Sloman, John. "How to Kick-Start a Faltering Economy the Keynes Way." BBC News Magazine. 22 October 2008, http://news.bbc.co.uk/2/hi/uk_news/magazine/7682887.stm.

Smith, David. *Mission After Christendom*. London: Darton, Longman & Todd, 2003.

Step Ahead. Accessed 10 November 2010, http://www.ywamthai.org/bangkok/stepahead.htm.

Step Ahead Integrated Community Development Foundation. *Vision, Mission, Values: Annual Report 2009–2010*. Bangkok: Step Ahead, 2010.

Stott, John. *Making Christ Known: Historic Mission Documents from the Lausanne Movement 1974–1989*. Grand Rapids: Eerdmans, 1996.

Sugden, Christopher. "Evangelicals and Wholistic Evangelism." In *Proclaiming Christ in Christ's Way: Studies in Integral Mission*, edited by Vinay Samuel and Albrecht Hauser, 29–51. Eugene: Wipf & Stock, 1989.

Supsin, Sriduda. "Microfinance." In *Vision, Mission, Values: Annual Report 2009–2010*. Step Ahead Integrated Community Development Foundation. Bangkok: Step Ahead, 2010.

United Nations. "We Can End Poverty: Millennium Development Goals and Beyond 2015." Accessed 6 November 2010, http://www.un.org/millenniumgoals/.

US Military Dictionary. "Priority." Answers. Accessed 15 March 2010, http://www.answers.com/topic/priority.

Walls, Andrew F. *The Missionary Movement in Christian History: Studies in the Transmission of Faith*. Edinburgh, T&T Clark, 1996.

Watson, David Lowes. "The Church As Journalist: Evangelism in the Context of the Local Church in the United States." *International Review of Mission* 72 (1983), 57–74.

Wilson, Kim. "The Moneylender's Dilemma." In *What's Wrong with Microfinance?* edited by Thomas Dichter and Malcolm Harper, 97–108. Rugby: Intermediate Technology Publications, 2007.

The World Bank. Accessed 26 March 2010, http://web.worldbank.org/WBSITE/EXTPOVERTY/0.print:Y.

World Bank Institute. "Basic Poverty Measurement and Analysis Course: Poverty Lines (Module 3)." Accessed 5 November 2010, http://info.worldbank.org/etools/docs/library/207203/Module3.pdf.

World Relief. Accessed 27 March 2010, http://worldrelief.org/mission-vision.

World Vision. Accessed 27 March 2010, www.wvi.org/.

Wright, Christopher J. H. *The Mission of God: Unlocking the Bible's Grand Narrative*. Downers Grove: IVP, 2006.

Wright, Nigel. *The Radical Evangelical*. London: SPCK, 1996.

Yamamori, Tetsunao, and Kenneth A. Eldred. *On Kingdom Business: Transforming Missions through Entrepreneurial Strategies.* Wheaton: Crossway, 2003.

Yunus, Mohammed. *Banker to the Poor: Micro-lending and the Battle against World Poverty.* New York: Public Affairs, 2007.

Langham
PARTNERSHIP

Langham Literature and its imprints are a ministry of Langham Partnership.

Langham Partnership is a global fellowship working in pursuit of the vision God entrusted to its founder John Stott –

> *to facilitate the growth of the church in maturity and Christ-likeness through raising the standards of biblical preaching and teaching.*

Our vision is to see churches in the majority world equipped for mission and growing to maturity in Christ through the ministry of pastors and leaders who believe, teach and live by the Word of God.

Our mission is to strengthen the ministry of the Word of God through:
- nurturing national movements for biblical preaching
- fostering the creation and distribution of evangelical literature
- enhancing evangelical theological education

especially in countries where churches are under-resourced.

Our ministry

Langham Preaching partners with national leaders to nurture indigenous biblical preaching movements for pastors and lay preachers all around the world. With the support of a team of trainers from many countries, a multi-level programme of seminars provides practical training, and is followed by a programme for training local facilitators. Local preachers' groups and national and regional networks ensure continuity and ongoing development, seeking to build vigorous movements committed to Bible exposition.

Langham Literature provides majority world preachers, scholars and seminary libraries with evangelical books and electronic resources through publishing and distribution, grants and discounts. The programme also fosters the creation of indigenous evangelical books in many languages, through writer's grants, strengthening local evangelical publishing houses, and investment in major regional literature projects, such as one volume Bible commentaries like *The Africa Bible Commentary* and *The South Asia Bible Commentary*.

Langham Scholars provides financial support for evangelical doctoral students from the majority world so that, when they return home, they may train pastors and other Christian leaders with sound, biblical and theological teaching. This programme equips those who equip others. Langham Scholars also works in partnership with majority world seminaries in strengthening evangelical theological education. A growing number of Langham Scholars study in high quality doctoral programmes in the majority world itself. As well as teaching the next generation of pastors, graduated Langham Scholars exercise significant influence through their writing and leadership.

To learn more about Langham Partnership and the work we do visit **langham.org**